Advance praise for *Surprises ar*

"More than a walk on the wild side, *Surprises around the Bend* captures the real essence of adventure that can be found only when we explore our world on foot. Theses stories inspire you to join with noted naturalists, writers, teachers, and seekers to find life as it is meant to be lived. Ditch the iPod, get off the boring treadmill, and free yourself from the same old rut of daily existence. I've found that true physical fitness requires you to discover the passion in living. Richard Hasler has found that passion, and his book will help you find it too. This is great reading to plan your next get-away with God, at home or beyond. Hasler's book is an insole for the soul providing real spiritual comfort for your next spiritual journey."

Brad Bloom
President, Lifestyle Media Group
Publisher, *Faith & Fitness Magazine*, faithandfitness.net

"*Surprises around the Bend* is truly an inspirational resource. All fifty stories are reminders that our journey starts with one step and that each new day is given to us as a precious gift to treasure."

Ardath H. Rodale
Chief Inspiration Officer, Rodale Inc.

"Our feet were made for walking and Richard Hasler convinces us that our soles are connected to our souls—feet and faith enhance each other. Yet walking is an imperiled spiritual practice. We are in danger of losing the necessity and the joy of moving on our own two feet. *Surprises around the Bend* shows us that walking still has much to teach us."

Arthur Paul Boers
Author of *The Way Is Made by Walking: A Pilgrimage along the Camino de Santiago*.

"One of the most practical books I have read in years. The depth of this resource restores our body, mind, and spirit as we enter the lives of great thinkers who have journeyed before us and discovered not only a footpath toward a deeper spiritual growth but found God in the very effort of the journey."

Tom P. Hafer
Author of *Faith and Fitness*

"Would you like to meet fifty fascinating world figures (in compact mini-biographies) and then even walk with them? Here is your book. Richard Hasler shows us through these walkers' stories how to walk ourselves and does so with a pastor's heart."

Frederick Dale Bruner
Professor of Theology Emeritus, Whitworth University

"You can walk, run, or saunter through this delightful book that brings to life the stories of well-known people who were passionate walkers. On your next walk you'll be encouraged, even inspired by this vast group of dignitaries you have joined. Read. Walk. Enjoy!"

Lauren Artress
Author of *Walking a Sacred Path: Rediscovering the Labyrinth as a Spiritual Practice*
and *The Sacred Path Companion: Using the Labyrinth to Heal and Transform*

"As a lifelong hiker, I was delighted with the way *Surprises around the Bend* uncovers new depth in a pursuit that has long fed my Christian faith. It is indeed a surprise to discover the great names of history who also found walking essential to their spiritual lives."

Ralph A. Boyer
Pastor, Christ Hamilton United Lutheran Church, Stroudsburg, Pennsylvania

1

SURPRISES

AROUND
the BEND

50 ADVENTUROUS WALKERS

Richard A. Hasler

Richard A. Hasler

Isaiah 40:31

Augsburg Books

Minneapolis

SURPRISES AROUND THE BEND
Fifty Adventurous Walkers

Scripture quotations are from the New Revised Standard Version Bible © 1989 Division of Christian Education of the National Council of the Churches of Christ in the United States of America. Used by permission.

Cover image: *Three Seasons* by Nicholas Wilton ©2007 Nicholas Wilton. Used by permission.
Cover design: Laurie Ingram
Book design: Jill Carroll Lafferty

Library of Congress Cataloging-in-Publication Data

Hasler, Richard A.
  Surprises around the bend : fifty adventurous walkers / Richard A. Hasler.
    p. cm.
  Includes bibliographical references.
  ISBN 978-0-8066-8041-5 (alk. paper)
  1. Spirituality. 2. Spiritual life—Christianity. 3. Walking—Religious aspects—Christianity. 4. Spiritual biography. I. Title.

BV4515.3.H37 2008
242—dc22   2007039647

The paper used in this publication meets the minimum requirements of American National Standard for Information Sciences—Permanence of Paper for Printed Library Materials, ANSI Z329.48-1984.

Manufactured in the U.S.A.

12   11   10   09   08   1   2   3   4   5   6   7   8   9   10

CONTENTS

ACKNOWLEDGMENTS

I want to express my gratitude to the following people who helped make this book possible.

I thank Linus Mundy, author of *The Complete Guide to Prayer-Walking*, whose encouragement came at just the right time. I am grateful to Linus for his permission to use "A Guided Prayer-Walk" (Extras).

I am indebted to Kevin Rosswurm, library director, and to all the librarians at the Cuyahoga Falls Library for their thoughtful and competent service in supplying me with indispensable books for my research through the interlibrary loan.

Numerous friends have given me support through the years both by their examples of diligent walking and their personal concern: William and Charlene Anderson, Arlin Bartholomew and Richard Geyer, Rev. Gordon and Wanda Bates, Rev. Ralph and Stephanie Boyer, Dr. Dale and Kathy Bruner, Dr. Dale and Claudia Duerr, Robert and Nancy Evans, Peg Feathers, Ron and Jill France, Rev. Dr. Roly and Margaret Fredericks, Dr. Paul and Eleanor Gertmenian, Ruth Hummel, Bill and Sandy Ignizio, Marti Klaus, Grace Lewis, Norman and Judy Lindblad, Lenore Lorenc, Beth Loresch, Fred and Becky Miller, Susan Morgan, Dr. William and Phyllis Peterson, Richard and Sandra Pech, William and Grace Schuettler, Rev. Robert and Jean Stokes, Rev. John and Mary Stoner, and Dr. Brian and Lisa Wind.

I have been fortunate to work with an outstanding church staff consisting of twenty dedicated people at the First Congregational Church, Hudson, Ohio, where I serve as a part-time associate pastor. In particular, I thank Rev. Dr. Peter Wiley, senior pastor, and Rev. Sue Ann Schmidt, associate pastor. Both of their families walk, not just for enjoyment but also in support of many worthwhile causes. I am also grateful to Karen Verner, parish nurse, for her Faithfully Fit Forever program, and to Dee Buchanan, director of children ministries, for the author photo.

David Oster, president, Laurel Lake Retirement Community, and all the wonderful residents with whom I work have shown me how our older years might be spent in vibrant and productive living.

The book would not have come to fruition without the expertise of the whole editorial staff of Augsburg Books. These talented people have taken my manuscript and made it so much better than the first draft. A special thank you to editor Henry "Hank" French for his astute editing, to Pamela Johnson, product manager, and to Bob Todd, publicist, for their work in sales and marketing. Most of all, I am indebted to senior editor Gloria Bengtson, who has guided me from the start with exceptionally fine suggestions that have sharpened the focus of the book. Her insights have been invaluable. All remaining errors, of course, are my own.

I owe much to my family for their constant support through the years. I wish to thank my daughter Karen, her husband Mike, and their three grown children, Michael, Katie, and Erin. (Karen read the manuscript and made many helpful comments.) I wish also to thank my son Rick, his wife Cindy, and their two grown children, Jennifer and Lindsay. (Rick supplied the walking programs that appear in "Extras.") Finally, I am especially grateful for my wife, Arlene, who has walked with me for more than fifty years. She has believed in me when I have not believed in myself. She has supplied keen observations during the writing process, and she remains my inspiration in all things.

INTRODUCTION

When Christmas season approaches our children do not have a difficult time deciding what to give me as a Christmas gift. When they come to my name on the list, they most likely say, "Give him a book. That will make him happy." They are right. There is nothing I enjoy more than reading a good book, especially a biography. A biography is a written account of a person's life. In a word, it is a story.

As I have read about famous men and women through the years, I have been struck by the fact that so many of our most creative people in history have been ardent walkers. Further, these same people testify that walking has played a significant role in their creativity. Still further, not a few of them have cited a particular walk that proved to be a serendipitous experience leading to personal transformation.

In the opening story, you will meet psychiatrist Carl Jung, who tells of receiving a ticket from his father when he was a young boy to ascend one of the highest mountains in the Swiss Alps and walk to his heart's content. In his words, "This was the best and most precious gift my father had given me."[1] In the last story you will meet Lutheran pastor and theologian Dietrich Bonhoeffer, an avid walker in his earlier years, who faced execution with peace and hope near the close of World War II at the Flossenburg concentration camp. He firmly believed that "death is the supreme festival on the road to freedom."

In between these two stories, you will encounter men and women, some believers, others not, who likewise affirm that walking had a salutary effect on their lives. People laughed when Abraham Lincoln went out for a walk. Even his closet friend remarked that Lincoln had no spring in his step. He "needed oiling." Nonetheless, near the close of the Civil War Lincoln led a walk of reconciliation through the streets of Richmond and no one laughed.

Emily Brontë grew up in what would seem to be the inhospitable environment of the desolate Yorkshire moors in northern England, and yet that place stimulated her imagination to write an unforgettable novel.

Toyohiko Kagawa, the Japanese mystic and social reformer, though confined to a tiny prison cell because he opposed Japanese imperialism during

World War II, developed a creative way of walking two miles in his cramped quarters.

Søren Kierkegaard, the Danish philosopher, strolled daily through the streets of his native Copenhagen talking to friends and strangers alike. It could be dangerous to walk with Kierkegaard, however, since as he hopped along he often made wild gestures with his arms and with the colorful umbrella he habitually carried with him.

Mother Teresa served as a contented teacher in India until one day she received "a call within a call" to work in the slums of Calcutta. But how was she to know if it was a genuine call? She decided to walk among "the poorest of the poor" for hours and hours. It was only then that she knew she had a real call.

One of James Michener's critics once quipped when asked about Michener's soon-to-be-published novel, "My best advice is don't read it, my second best is don't drop it on your foot." Michener wrote a number of big books that became best sellers and he always claimed that when his writing went poorly it was because he had not been walking enough.

C. S. Lewis, arguably the leading evangelical of the twentieth century, walked each afternoon and more so on holidays. His conversion is frequently described as instantaneous. Lewis, however, asserted that hours of walking one night, circling Addison's Walk at Oxford with two of his colleagues discussing faith and doubt, had a lot to do with his conversion.

These companions of the way are the ones I turn to when I am tired and sluggish and want to slack off on my regular walking. Their examples embolden me to continue in the right direction.

I am technically retired as a pastor but I remain active, working part-time on a church staff and continuing to do freelance writing. I usually walk around my neighborhood. When the weather is bad I go to the indoor track at the state-of-the-art Natatorium in our city of Cuyahoga Falls, Ohio. When the weather is good I am apt to meander along the trails in the nearby Cuyahoga Valley National Park or in the numerous Metro Parks in Summit County in northeast Ohio. I am fond of visiting the F. A. Seiberling Naturealm, with its 104-acre nature center and arboretum, and hiking in the Sand Run Metro Park. The Cleveland-Akron area provides a rich variety of walking sites. On vacation trips I welcome the opportunity to hike in many of the great national parks scattered around our beautiful land.

Some years ago my wife, Arlene, and I participated in a Rotary Club exchange with Rotarians in the Midlands of England. We spent two delightful weeks with them. Before the trip began, I completed a form indicating my interests and what I would like to see in England. I happened to mention "walking and history." The first couple we stayed with, a young architect and his wife, an elementary school teacher, lived in the medieval town of Oundle.

On the second day of our visit, they took me on a ten-mile hike through the picturesque Northamptonshire countryside to a historic site they wished me to observe.

As we approached Lyveden, I saw high on a distant hill what appeared to be a magnificent manor house. When we arrived at the spot, however, I was disappointed to see that the roof was missing and much of the rest of the building was unfinished. Then the couple told me the story of Sir Thomas Tresham who, in the last part of the seventeenth century, had the dream of building a spectacular cruciform manor house to reflect his faith. Changing political conditions and mounting debts forced him to abandon his plans midcourse. That day was the beginning of a wonderful fortnight that included many fascinating episodes of "walking and history."

Three years ago, Arlene and I spent nine days in Switzerland, one of the most memorable trips we have ever taken. I had a personal interest in going to Switzerland because, in 1749, the first members of my father's family came to Philadelphia from Switzerland. We did a lot of walking in this indescribably gorgeous country, but we did nothing like the arduous mountain climbing and lengthy hikes taken by Jung, Kübler Ross, Goethe, Dickens, and others mentioned in this book. Just being in the majestic Alps, however, and sauntering alongside the numerous pristine lakes helped me to identify with—and heighten my appreciation for—the many creative walkers who have come to this region through the years.

In my preaching, teaching, and in other pastoral contacts, I am keenly aware that what many people remember most of all are the stories, the biblical stories of course, and also the historical and contemporary stories that connect with their life situations. This book is about such stories.

The walking motif permeates the biblical story. Jesus was a walker. Someone is bound to say, "Well, everyone walked in those days. That was the only mode of transportation. Jesus did not have an SUV at his disposal." But such common-sense knowledge is not exactly true. People with authority and power tended to ride on horses or camels. They frequently were driven by servants in chariots, in carriages, and in other conveyances.

Jesus had a different understanding of power and authority. His servant ministry took him where the common people were in the villages and by the lakeside. Furthermore, he seemed to marvel at the natural beauty all around him, noticing the lilies of the field and the birds of the air.

The disciples had mixed emotions as they followed him. Mark explains in his Gospel: "They were on the road, going up to Jerusalem, and Jesus was walking ahead of them; they were amazed, and those who followed were afraid" (Mark 10:32). In other words, his followers were both excited and scared to be with Jesus, the one who walked before them.

I have found it to be both exciting and scary to be a Christian disciple, a follower of the Way. Jesus' call to discipleship is certainly the most satisfying and meaningful challenge I could ever have. On the other hand, I am aware of how far short I fall in responding to the cost of discipleship. For example, the life of prayer is central to my spiritual pilgrimage, and yet prayer is difficult for me. I feel I am still a beginner in the practice of prayer. What helps me the most is prayer-walking. When I am out on the open road something happens I cannot fully explain, but somehow God seems close at hand, and I am able to pray. The insights of all the creative walkers whose stories fill the pages of this book have been of assistance to me in one way or another, but if I have a favorite instructor it would be Frank Laubach. He teaches me to practice the presence of God as I walk, and in all situations in life to shoot "flash" intercessory prayers toward everyone I meet along the way.

At the beginning of each story in this book you will find a scripture reading to lead you into the story. At the end of each story you will find a "Thought to Ponder" and a prayer to help you integrate the insights from each story into your own life.

Lest you be intimidated by extraordinary men and women and say you cannot emulate them, listen to what Dr. Gene D. Cohen has to tell us. Using the insights of Harvard professor Howard Gardner, he cites two kinds of creativity—creativity with a "big C" and creativity with a "little c." The former applies to exceptional people like Albert Einstein, an enthusiastic hiker, who developed the theory of relativity, dramatically changing the way we look at the universe today. Creativity with a "little c" applies to the creativity of ordinary people when they do something unique, whether it be writing a clear memo, designing an art object, making a meal from scratch, or simply approaching a problem from a fresh perspective.[2]

Dr. Michael Roizen, heart specialist at the Cleveland Clinic, contends that "even thirty minutes of walking a day works miracles."[3] Roizen, of course, is thinking primarily of the special benefits walking provides for physical fitness. In addition, millions of people, young and old, are walking steadily today, not only to gain and maintain physical fitness but also to seek mental renewal and even spiritual rejuvenation.

Lauren Artress, canon for special ministries at Grace Cathedral in San Francisco, has reintroduced the twelfth-century walking meditation of the labyrinth, deepening the spiritual life of countless people throughout the world. Nor should we forget the throngs who walk together to raise funds for cancer research, to seek a cure for diabetes or other life-threatening diseases, to stop hunger, to protest racial discrimination, and to support many other worthy causes.

How do you get started—or restarted—on your own road to shalom, or wholeness of life? *First, you must prepare.* Ardath Rodale, writing in her book *Gifts of the Spirit,* tells of her daily walk along the ocean path while vacationing on the island of Maui, Hawaii. One morning she looked across the bay and saw "a huge, fat, vibrant rainbow!" She came upon a mother and daughter also out for a walk. The mother, who had her head down while she talked, never noticed the rainbow until Ardath brought it to her attention.[4]

You need to be prepared, always anticipating that there may be gifts all around you, if only you have eyes to see. Preparation begins with a sense of expectancy.

Second, you must persevere. Former Notre Dame football coach Lou Holtz, in his book *A Teen's Game Plan for Life,* writes about one of his players, Mike Brennan, who was the slowest football player he had ever seen. The players nicknamed him "Turtle." But Holtz, who did not like that expression, remarked, "I thought that was very disparaging to the turtle."[5] Nevertheless, Brennan persevered and he found a way to use his strengths to offset his slowness. Eventually, he became a varsity player at Notre Dame and played for four years in the National Football League.

You must learn to persevere and not give up when walking becomes tiring or boring. If the creative walkers in this book teach us anything it is that endurance is something that can be learned through consistent practice. Nothing can be more satisfying than to learn the art of LSD: long, slow, distance walking.

Third, you need to personalize. Daniel Pink, in his provocative book *A Whole New Mind,* relates the story of a man who goes into a first-grade class and asks, "How many artists are there in the room?" All the kids raise their hands. He repeats the question to second-graders, and about three-fourths of the children lift up their hands. When he asks the sixth-graders the same question, however, not a single hand goes up.

Apparently, it does not take long to convince ourselves that we are not artists or, at least, that we do not want to admit that we are artists. Pink concludes that no matter what field we enter today, we must cultivate an artistic sensibility. He argues, "We may not all be Deli or Degas. But today we must all be designers."[6]

The challenge for you is to design your own walking style and program. Do not copy slavishly what someone else is doing. Each of the fifty creative walkers we will examine in this book was different in some respect from the others, and yet each one demonstrated unusual creativity in his or her particular field. You can do the same.

You will find in the "Extras" section in the back of the book a couple of practical walking programs that can be adapted to your own personal needs. See what suits you, and use it to design your own walking pattern.

You have choices to make concerning how you live your life. Pressures will be brought to bear on you by individuals and institutions to do it their way, but their way may not be the best path for you to follow. It is easy to be misled. You need companions and role models who have experienced obstacles similar to those you have known in your own life and yet have overcome those obstacles to become vibrant and creative people.

If you accept the invitation to follow in the footsteps of these exemplars, you too may one day breathe what Wallace Stevens inhaled—"the deep woods-coolness." You might come to know what Brenda Ueland was talking about when she said that as she walked she felt "the little inward bombs bursting quietly." You may even exult in traveling Thomas Merton's "road to joy." In a word, surprises, even miracles, await you around the bend.

PHYSICIANS
&
NATURALISTS

The Most Precious Gift

Carl Jung (1875-1961)

You show me the path of life.
In your presence there is fullness of joy;
in your right hand are pleasures forevermore.

PSALM 16:11

The young boy and his father stood at the base of the mighty Rigi in the Swiss Alps. The boy could not believe he was there on vacation with his father. They do not usually share intimacies. Carl, the son, realized his father was an honored pastor in the village, but he suspected his father's real love was his theological and linguistic books and not his parish responsibilities. Carl wanted something different from life. He desired to be moved by a great passion. His heart was often stirred as if something or someone was speaking to him beyond his own consciousness.

Carl, fourteen, and his father left their home near Basel; they traveled to Lucerne, boarded a steamboat, and sailed across the lake to Vitznau. Above the town rose the gigantic Rigi. Decision time had come. Carl's father did not have enough money for two tickets, but he did have enough for one. Pressing the ticket in his son's hand, he urged him to board the cogwheel railway and go up to the summit of the mountain.

Speechless with joy, Carl ascended the steep incline. He brought with him a bamboo cane and an English jockey cap that he thought were the proper attire for the occasion. When he arrived at the top in the thin air he looked for miles in every direction. He had never seen anything like it. Here there were no teachers or school—he was on his own. He walked carefully, following marked paths because tremendous precipices surrounded him.

Ecstasy flooded his soul. Writing as an old man in his autobiography *Memories*, he recalled, "It was all very solemn, and I felt one had to be polite and silent up here, for one was in God's world. . . . This was the best and most precious gift my father had ever given me."[1]

Carl Jung would grow up to be one of the most famous psychiatrists in the world. In his early career he was associated with Sigmund Freud, the eminent psychiatrist from Vienna, but eventually Jung broke away from Freud and developed his own approach to analytical psychology. He pioneered theories of personality and the unconscious and he gave us terms we still use today such as *introvert* and *extrovert, anima* and *animus,* to name just a few.

Throughout his lifetime Jung was an avid walker. He hiked from his village of Klein-Heningen to the city of Basel, a one-and-a-half-hour trip one way, first as a high school student and later as a university student. As a young adult he took long walks in Germany's Black Forest, not far from Basel. When he became a practicing psychiatrist in Zurich, it was common to see him walking the streets or strolling along the side of the lake. Medical student Elisabeth Kübler Ross recalls seeing Jung on his frequent promenades, but she was too shy at that time to speak to him. Even when Jung counseled his patients, especially when he analyzed their dreams, he paced back and forth. He liked to be on the move, whether indoors or outdoors.

Despite Jung's lifelong practice of walking by the lake or in the dark forest, nothing compared to that extraordinary vacation day as a teenager when he had the sensation of "walking in God's world." Deirdre Bair, Jung's most recent biographer, had many conversations with friends who knew Jung, and they all attest: "Throughout his adult life, whenever he was exhausted from overwork or stress, he would conjure up the image of himself at the peak of this mountain."[2]

Indeed, the memory of that vacation trip stayed with Jung forever—the best and most precious gift his father had ever given him.

Thought to Ponder

If you have had an experience of "walking in God's world," describe your feelings and share them with someone else.

Prayer

Lord, help me to walk in the midst of your creation with eyes wide open and give you praise for the glory that surrounds me. Amen.

Alpine landscapes of soaring peaks, meadows, and lakes attract hikers and adventure sports enthusiasts to Switzerland. A well-organized and scrupulously maintained network of many thousands of miles of trails provide experienced and novice hikers with abundant choice. Tourist offices are well stocked with maps and have route information readily available.

Robert Strauss
Adventure Trekking

FROM COAST TO COAST

David Livingstone (1813-1873)

For you have delivered my soul from death,
and my feet from falling,
so that I may walk before God
in the light of life.

PSALM 56:13

The tall slender Scottish medical missionary slumped in dejection, unable to pray or continue his work. He had come to South Africa with high expectations but, after twelve years on the mission field, he had only one convert to show for his indefatigable efforts. What should he do? Should he return to Scotland a failure? He did love the African people, but for some reason he was unable to communicate the Christian gospel to them.

Born in Blantyre, Scotland, in 1813, David Livingstone was forced at an early age to work in the local cotton mill because of his family's dire financial circumstances. His tremendous workload left little time for play, though he did walk occasionally in the countryside, and he read widely when time permitted. Many people did not consider him to be very sociable.

Working as a "piecer" in the cotton mill, Livingstone's job was to piece together threads that might be ready to break on the spinning frames. Biographer Tim Jeal explains why the piecers' tasks were not easy: "Piecers walked up to twenty miles a day in the mills and much of this distance was covered crawling or stooping."[3] Unpleasant as these tasks were, they prepared David for even more challenging treks years later through the African jungles.

As a young man Livingstone began to take the Christian faith seriously and contemplated preparing to become a medical missionary. He studied medicine at Anderson College in Glasgow, and at the same time he made application to the London Missionary Society. There were obstacles, however. He found studying Hebrew and Greek, the original languages of the Bible, both unappealing and impractical. Furthermore, his early practice preaching was atrocious, so much so that some members of the congregation refused to attend worship when they heard Livingstone was scheduled to preach.

Nonetheless, Livingstone felt God had called him to prepare for a mission assignment. He completed his medical degree in 1840, and he was ordained to preach the gospel. He originally intended to go to China, but when that door closed he accepted a call to South Africa.

Livingstone arrived at Cape Town and headed north to Kuruman where Robert Moffat had established a mission base. Livingstone had previously met Moffat in Scotland, and he knew of his pioneer mission work.

Before long, Livingstone would marry Moffat's daughter, Mary, who would bear him five children. Their marriage was not a happy one. Livingstone was domineering and not in tune with his wife's emotional needs, especially as he became obsessed with his mission objectives. Only in the last few years of their marriage did Livingstone show much sensitivity to his wife and his children.

After twelve years in South Africa, Livingstone felt he was an absolute failure. Although he loved the black people of South Africa, he could not relate the Christian message to them. After much self-searching and prayer, he decided that maybe God had indeed called him to the mission field but to do something different from the evangelistic work at which, he himself admitted, he was totally inadequate.

Livingstone perceived his new calling to be that of an explorer who would open up the rather unknown African continent to Christian missionaries who would come one day and do what he had been unable to do; namely, preach the gospel effectively. Further, he desired to bring not only Christianity but also British civilization to the native peoples. Still further, he sought to find ways and means to eliminate the abominable slave trade.

To accomplish this threefold aim, he believed he must find a "missionary path" for people to travel "from coast to coast" through the jungle. Oliver Ransford, in *David Livingstone: The Dark Interior,* quotes Livingstone as vowing: "I shall open a path into the interior or perish."[4]

Despite personal illnesses (malaria and other diseases), conflicts with indigenous peoples, attacks by wild animals, and travel on dangerous trails, he pressed on to follow his vision. Eventually, he became the first white man to walk (over four years) through four thousand miles of uncharted land. He returned home a hero. After a while he returned to Africa, this time sponsored by the Royal Geographic Society, with the commission to explore the Zambesi River. He encountered numerous obstacles in attempting to navigate

> Trekking *comes from the* Dutch trekken *(to draw or travel). A trek is an arduous, slow journey.*
>
> *Gary D. Yanker*
> The Complete Book of Exercise Walking

Today, as always when I am afoot in the woods, I feel the possibility, the reasonableness, the practicality of living in the world in a way that would enlarge rather than diminish the hope of life.

Wendell Berry
"An Entrance
to the Woods,"
Recollected Essays

the river, but in the end he created excellent maps of Central Africa that proved valuable tools for the missionaries who followed him.

After a brief period at home, in 1866 Livingstone returned to Africa, this time with the intent to find the source of the Nile River. He was seriously ill throughout much of the exploration. On May 1, 1873, two of Livingstone's servants found him kneeling beside his bed as if he was praying. On closer inspection, they found him dead. His body was carried across the continent by devoted Africans, and he was later buried in London's Westminster Abbey.

David Livingstone was a complex figure—medical doctor, missionary, and explorer, the first white man to open up the mysteries of black Africa to the Western world. Although frustrated in his original evangelistic work, he found new ways to serve God as an explorer. To accomplish his dream, he walked "from coast to coast" at great sacrifice to himself.

Thought to Ponder

If you are presently faced with a "closed door" as was David Livingstone, what new thing do you think God has prepared for you?

Prayer

Faithful God, be with me in the time of difficult decisions when I know not which way to turn. Lead me into a fresh adventure along your sure path. Amen.

NATURE'S FIRST EXERCISE

George Sheehan (1918-1993)

*And when you turn to the right or when you
turn to the left, your ears shall hear a word behind you,
saying, "This is the way; walk in it."*

ISAIAH 30:21

Dr. George Sheehan once described what happens when he is about to begin a race: "Before I even park the car, I can feel the adrenalin flowing. The sight of runners warming up sends a rush through my bowels. The smell of the dressing room sets my pulse to racing. The track under my feet makes me break out in a cold sweat."[5]

Is that how we feel when we engage in a sport? Do we have this sense of anticipation when we come to worship? Are we passionate about anything we do? Sheehan believed in the strenuous life. He was determined to go all out for the tape.

You may think that I have made a mistake in including Sheehan in this collection of creative walkers. Was he not the well-known guru of runners during the 1970s and 1980s? Yes, cardiologist and marathon runner Sheehan was a leading authority on running and racing, but he had some good words to say about the value of walking, too.

First let us examine the highlights of his extraordinary life. Born in Brooklyn in 1918, Sheehan grew up in a physician's home with thirteen brothers and sisters. He excelled in academics and became a track star at Manhattan College. He trained to be a cardiologist, and later served in World War II with the Navy in the South Pacific. He and his wife, the former Mary Jane Fleming, had a large family of their own including twelve children.

Although successful as a doctor, with the passing years he neglected his own health. He became a couch potato. When he was about forty-five years old he decided to change his lifestyle. He returned to his early love of running; in fact, he ran every spare moment he had. He reserved at least one hour each day to run. In a short time, he was running thirty miles every week. He competed in more than fifty marathons, including the famed Boston Marathon.

RACE WALKING: As of this writing, the male record for the mile is 5:33.50, held by an American, Tim Lewis. The female record is 6:16.72, held by Sada Eidikite, Soviet Union. Most people can't even run that fast flat out. These race-walking records are remarkable athletic achievements.

Casey Meyers
Walking

At the same time, he was reading the Greek philosophers and the fathers and mystics of the Christian church. He used his fresh intellectual and spiritual insights to help him interpret the world of exercise and sports. He began to inspire others to hit the road and listen to their bodies. Before long, he was asked to write columns in running magazines—for twenty-five years he wrote a column in *Runner's World*. Later, he became the author of best-selling books. In 1986, Sheehan was diagnosed with prostate cancer. He battled the disease for seven years before dying in 1993, at the age of seventy-four.

Although he had always had an appreciation for walking, it was not until later in life, when he no longer was able to run, that he began to walk consistently. In the foreword to Casey Meyer's book *Walking: A Complete Guide to the Complete Exercise*, Sheehan wrote: "All exercises are good exercises if you know how to use them. And of all these exercises, walking has the longest history, the best pedigree, the most distinguished practitioners. Walking was Nature's first exercise."[6]

One walk in particular taught Sheehan a lesson about the relationship between walking and running. As he was out for an ambitious walk one day, he noticed a runner friend approaching him. He raised his hand to greet him, but the man ran right by him without even recognizing him. He barely gave him a glance. Sheehan mused, "Yet if I were running, I know I would get a friendly word, at least a wave."[7]

This slight caused Sheehan to explore the world of walking even more than he had in his earlier years. He remembered that some of the best track coaches he had known always combined walking with running in their conditioning programs, and the more he thought about it he remembered that the amount of time spent walking usually exceeded that spent running. Walking is an excellent way to lose weight. Furthermore, no matter what sport you might be training for, walking is the primary exercise applicable to all.

Then Sheehan began to think not just about physical fitness but also about mental renewal. He realized, now that he was walking more than running, that, "I come up with as many good ideas as I do on a run."[8] From his comprehensive reading he recalled that ancient Greek philosophers walked

while they taught in their so-called peripatetic schools. He marveled that the English poet William Wordsworth was purported to have logged no less than 175,000 miles during his life.

Considering the spiritual realm, Sheehan readily admitted that walking was a superior way to handle stress, was conducive to meditation, and opened up all kinds of creative opportunities. In the end, this popular authority on running amazingly declared, "The walker has found the peace the runner still seeks."9

Walkers are not fanatics like other sports or exercise enthusiasts. Walking itself calms you down and gives you an even-handed view of life and exercise.

Gary D. Yanker
The Complete Book of
Exercise Walking

Thought to Ponder

Reflect upon the "many good ideas" that you have received from your own daily walks.

Prayer

God of light and wisdom, may I not look down upon walking or anything else because it appears to be simple. Teach me your way, and I will follow your light. Amen.

Long Hikes in the Mountains

Elisabeth Kübler Ross (1926-2004)

*…but those who wait for the LORD shall renew their
strength, they shall mount up with wings like eagles,
they shall run and not be weary,
they shall walk and not faint.*

ISAIAH 40:31

Who at her birth would have given the two-pound girl much of a chance of survival in 1926, let alone the prospect of becoming one of the most prominent physicians of the twentieth century? But Elisabeth Kübler Ross, born the first of triplets in Zurich, Switzerland, on July 8, 1926, fooled everyone.

Kübler Ross had help along the way, and no one inspired her more than her father in overcoming every adversity she faced. While his three daughters were still young, he took them on long hikes in the mountains. She gradually built up her physical strength, and even more, her spirit soared as she followed her father on exciting, even dangerous, expeditions amid the splendor of the Swiss Alps. Her father would point out half-hidden edelweiss in a rock or a rare alpine flower. He led his children through thick forests and open meadows. These outdoor experiences left an indelible mark on Elisabeth and influenced her adult years.

Christmas Day always was a special time for the children. Their father invariably would take them for a hike in the woods that lasted for several hours. He would tell them that they were searching for the Christ child. They never did see signs of him. Returning home exhausted, Elisabeth and her sisters would be delighted to see in the meantime that the Christ child had come to their home while they were away, and they found gift packages everywhere. The spectacular day ended with the singing of Christmas carols and their father reading the Christmas story.[10]

When Elisabeth and her two sisters were confirmed by their Swiss Reformed pastor, as was the custom, each confirmand was given a personal scripture verse. The three girls received the verse 1 Corinthians 13:13: "And now faith, hope, and love abide, these three; and the greatest of these is love." Her two sisters received the words *faith* and *hope* and Elisabeth received the word *love*—a fitting symbol for the one who later would exhibit unique compassion in her caring work as a physician to the dying.

After graduation from medical school in Zurich, Kübler Ross practiced for a while as a country physician. Sometime later, she and her husband, also a physician, moved to New York City. Still later, the couple moved to the Chicago area where Kübler Ross became interested in the subject of death and dying. As she visited in the cancer wards of a great metropolitan hospital, she realized that most of the other physicians paid little attention to terminally ill patients. She decided to listen to their stories, and in the process, she learned that they had much to teach her. As a result, she wrote the pioneer study *Death and Dying* in 1969, and forged a whole new way of relating to terminally ill patients. She theorized that people close to death tend to go through five stages of grief: denial, anger, bargaining, depression, and acceptance. In a word, she taught Americans how to talk about death. The thriving hospice movement in our nation owes much to her.

> *Any account of the Alps must lead sooner or later to the events of July 1865. In that month an obscure printer named Edward Whymper became Europe's most talked-about man. The reason? He had climbed the Matterhorn, one of the world's legendary mountains and one of the last to be conquered in the Alps. But he had earned his glory at a horrible cost. A rope snapped during the descent and four of his seven-strong team fell to their deaths.*
>
> Fergus Fleming
> Killing Dragons:
> The Conquest of the Alps

Although living comfortably in a Chicago suburb during the 1970s, at times Kübler Ross would grow restless. The blandness and sameness of suburban life suffocated her. She yearned to be hiking in her adored mountains. Most of all, she desired that her children would have the same outdoor adventures that thrilled her as a child.

One day she could stand it no longer. She packed up her children and boarded a flight to Switzerland. Her mother met her at the charming village of Zermatt, at the base of the majestic Matterhorn, and soon they were off hiking in the Alps. In her autobiography, *The Wheel of Life: A Memoir of Living and Dying,* she explains what she passionately wished for her children:

> I wanted them to know what it was like to get up early in the morning, hike in the hills and mountains, appreciate the flowers, the different grasses, the crickets and butterflies. I wanted them to gather wildflowers and colorful rocks during the day and then at night let the stars fill their heads with dreams.[11]

Walking in the great outdoors always stimulated Kübler Ross physically, mentally, and spiritually. As a result, she met everything that came her way with confidence, and she wanted this same personal renewal for her children.

We may not be able to jet off to Switzerland as easily as Elisabeth Kübler Ross did, but we can go somewhere closer to home in the great outdoors and know the liberating sense of walking away the blues.

Thought to Ponder

Where can you go to find the personal renewal that Dr. Kübler Ross desired for her children? Could you go to the mountains, the seashore, or some other place?

Prayer

O God, I wish for myself what Elisabeth Kübler Ross desired for her children, "to gather wildflowers and colorful rocks during the day," and then at night to let the stars fill my head with dreams. May it be so, gracious Lord. Amen.

American Indians are a people especially aware of the Great Spirit found in nature. The sun, wind, trees, mountains, and animals manifested God, while nature provided the best place where the Great Spirit could be experienced.

Philip Ferranti
Hiking: The Ultimate Natural Prescription for Health and Wellness

Sauntering in a Strange Country

Henry David Thoreau (1817-1862)

Better the poor walking in integrity
than one perverse of speech who is a fool.

PROVERBS 19:1

Henry David Thoreau was not an easy man to like. He was stubborn, unorthodox, and independent of spirit. He despised the rising industrialism in his Massachusetts village of Concord. Everyday work bored him. His response to the kind of life that most everyone took for granted was to "drop out" of society, at least for short periods of time. He sought the simple life in the natural world. In his own words, "Two or three hours of walking will carry me to as strange a country as I expect to see."[12]

Graduating from Harvard in 1838, he determined to march to the beat of a different drummer. He preferred to amble around his beloved Walden Pond. As a young man he lived in the home of Ralph Waldo Emerson, the noted essayist and transcendentalist philosopher, who shared his love of walking. The transcendentalists believed that when people were born they already had a certain knowledge of what was good and true. If people, no matter how old, even young children, lived simple lives, they would hear an inner voice showing them the way to go.

Later, in 1845, Thoreau moved outside of town to Walden Pond where he lived in primitive surroundings, walking and observing nature, talking with strangers, and meditating upon ideas that later would be incorporated into his writing and that would remain popular even to our own time.

Thoreau wrote *A Week on the Concord and Merrimack Rivers* (1849) and *Walden* (1854). Still later, after his death, previously unpublished books based on his various trips were also published, such as *Excursions* (1863), *The Maine Woods* (1864), *Cape Cod* (1865), and *A Yankee in Canada* (1866).

Walden, his most influential book, celebrated the life of simplicity and has become a classic study of nature for succeeding generations. If we are looking for Thoreau's specific views on walking, however, we turn to his essay simply titled "Walking."

He used the word *sauntering* to describe the type of walking he did. Sauntering has its origins among medieval pilgrims who traveled to the Holy Land

Sometime in August Rousseau was on the road again, and despite all of these disappointments he remembered the journey as a happy one. In fact sedentary life always depressed him, and the physical rhythm of tramping along the highway felt liberating and even inspiring.

Leo Damrosch
Jean-Jacques Rousseau:
Restless Genius

(a la *Sainte Terre*). Children seeing such wayfarers would exclaim, "There goes a *Sainte-Terrer*"—a Saunterer, a Holy Lander. Thoreau employed the term to differentiate his style of walking from mere physical exercise. He was not into "swinging dumbbells."[13]

Thoreau believed he had been born into a family of walkers. He could not buy such an experience and he attributed his good fortune to the grace of God. He summed up his regimen of walking as follows: "I think that I cannot preserve my health and spirits, unless I spend four hours a day at least—and it is commonly more than that—sauntering through the woods and over the hills and fields, absolutely free from all worldly engagements."[14]

Thoreau simply could not understand how mechanics and shopkeepers in his village could work all day long in cramped positions without spending time wandering in the natural world. He wondered why they had not committed suicide long ago. On the contrary, though he went out every day, he never exhausted his trails through the woods. His day was filled with one bright prospect after another in this strange country.

What impact did Thoreau's daily treks through the woods have upon his writing? His close friend Emerson gives us a hint when he comments in his journal: "The length of his walk uniformly made the length of his writing. If shut up in the house, he did not write at all."[15]

Emerson also paid high tribute to Thoreau when he wrote:

> It was a pleasure and a privilege to walk with him. He knew the country like a fox or a bird, and passed it as freely by paths of his own. He knew every track in the snow or in the ground, and what creature had taken his path before him. One must submit abjectly to such a guide and the reward was great.[16]

Each day Thoreau could see the activities of the villagers in the distance, but he did not envy them. Every sunset emboldened him to travel westward in the spirit of the great pioneers, and so he sauntered on toward the Holy Land, toward his goal of the free and simple life.

Thought to Ponder

How does your daily discipline of walking compare with Thoreau's?

Prayer

Everlasting God, grant me the courage of someone like Thoreau to walk to the beat of a different drummer. Instill in me the discipline to go apart from the crowd and know your renewing presence in the world of nature. Amen.

WALKING SYNONYMS

slink
slither
stalk
shuffle
slog
trudge
hike
stroll
strut
swagger
promenade
gallivant
jaunt
mosey
wander
peregrinate
amble
saunter

Joseph A. Amato
On Foot

CLIMB THE MOUNTAINS AND GET THEIR GOOD TIDINGS

John Muir (1834-1914)

Get you up to a high mountain, O Zion,
herald of good tidings;
lift up your voice with strength.

ISAIAH 40:9

Young John Muir, growing up in Scotland, learned the Bible the hard way. His cruel father severely beat him until he memorized the whole New Testament and most of the Old Testament, in John's own words, "by sore flesh."[17] The family moved to America in 1849, where John's father continued to insist on a strict pattern of Bible reading and prayer in his home. The elder Muir had become even more fanatical about his religious beliefs and devoted all his waking hours to Bible reading, peering out the window of his Wisconsin home from time to time to be sure that John and his brothers were properly tending to the farm chores.

In 1860, Muir left home to attend the University of Wisconsin. His father gave him no encouragement or financial support, but Muir was skilled with inventions related to clocks, thermometers, and other practical appliances, and in this way he was able to pay his bills. At the university he took only courses that appealed to him, and he never completed his degree. New worlds opened to him, and botany in particular fascinated him.

Muir felt a call to the world of nature. On his first journey he took with him the poems of Robert Burns, John Milton's *Paradise Lost,* and the New Testament— but before long books became secondary to him. Is it any wonder, after his father's inhuman method of study accompanied by corporal punishment, that Muir would turn from the world of books to the world of nature? He was determined to look for God in the splendor and wonder of the divine creation.

If ever there was a walker with a totally free spirit it was John Muir. He confessed that the only thing he

Of those who have written of nature surpassingly well . . . John Muir was the wildest. He was the most active, the most at home in the wilderness, the most daring, the most capable, the most self-reliant.

Edwin Way Teale, editor
The Wilderness World of John Muir

needed to begin his walking adventure was to "throw some tea and bread in an old sack and jump over the back fence."[18] He went into the American wilderness on foot, alone, without a gun, with limited supplies, and explored the beauty of this great land.

After leaving the University of Wisconsin, Muir walked a thousand miles from Indiana through Kentucky, Tennessee, and Georgia until he reached his final destination in Florida. It was to be an exceptional walk that changed his life and motivated him to walk westward. Later, he went to California. He was the pioneer explorer in the gorgeous Yosemite Valley. In his journal he exclaimed, "Never before had I seen so glorious a landscape, so boundless an affluence of sublime mountain beauty. The most extravagant description I might give of this view to any one who has not seen similar landscapes with his own eyes would not so much as hint at its grandeur and the spiritual glow that covered it."[19]

In the last half of the nineteenth century, John Muir was our most intrepid and worshipful explorer of the western extremities of our North American continent. For decades he tramped up and down through our God-created wonders, from the California Sierras to the Alaskan glaciers, observing, reporting, praising, and experiencing—entering into whatever he found with childlike delight and mature reverence.

Eugene Peterson
in Philip Yancey's
Church. Why Bother?

Muir was sometimes criticized for overworking such adjectives as *glorious* in describing the beauty of the land he saw for the first time. He once wrote a friend that he was busy slaughtering *gloriouses* in his manuscript. But as Edwin Way Teale, an editor of Muir's writings and a superb naturalist himself, comments, the overworking of this adjective revealed something of the man's character, "For him, always, the world *was* glorious."[20]

Muir championed the conservation movement to preserve great natural treasures such as Yosemite. He lobbied President Theodore Roosevelt to use his so-called "bully pulpit" to guarantee protection of America's natural environment, paving the way for today's stupendous national park system. He was president of the Sierra Club from its inception in 1892 until his death in 1914. This activist organization continues to set the pace in the conservationist movement today.

In his journal, Muir once penned these words: "I only went out for a walk and finally concluded to stay out till sundown, for going out, I found, I was really going in."[21] His external walks always seemed to provide inner revitalization for him wherever he wandered.

Perhaps the best summary of his personal philosophy is found in his exhortation, "Climb the mountains and get their good tidings. Nature's peace will flow into you as sunshine flows into trees. The winds will blow their freshness into you, and the storms their energy, while cares will drop off like leaves."[22]

Thought to Ponder

Is God's world of nature as "glorious" to you as it was to John Muir? Why or why not?

Prayer

Lord of all the seasons, awaken me to see the beauty of your universe, and may I too "climb the mountains and get their good tidings." Amen.

THIS HAPPY TRAVELER

Francis of Assisi (1182-1226)

As you go, proclaim the good news,
"The kingdom of heaven has come near."

MATTHEW 10:7

Francis sweeps clean with a primitive broom his little church, Santa Maria degli Angeli, at Portiuncula in the woods. It is Saint Matthias's Day. He awaits the coming of the priest who is to say mass in this church he has just refurbished. Francis will be the server. The gospel for the day accents the story of Jesus sending out his disciples to preach and heal in his name. At the close of the passage Francis hears Jesus say, "Take no gold, or silver, or copper in your belts, no bags for your journey, or two tunics, or sandals, or a staff; for laborers deserve their food" (Matthew 10:9-10).

Those words hit Francis like a thunderbolt. Now, he knows what he is to do—follow Jesus in this simple, humble, sacrificial way, sharing the good news of the kingdom. To make sure he has heard God's Word correctly, he goes to the priest at the conclusion of the service and asks him to explain the scriptural passage in more depth. The priest obliges and Francis no longer doubts his calling as he begins a new adventure of faith.

Francis, born in Assisi, Italy, in 1182, was reared in a prosperous home. As a young boy he was known for his joyful and generous demeanor. When he became a young man he developed an intense desire to win glory as a soldier but, during a battle between the town of Assisi and the neighboring city of Perugia, he was captured and imprisoned. Once free from jail, he vowed to fight in military service for the Pope, but soon after he decided he should simply serve Christ the Lord.

Francis spent much time in prayer and as a result he found himself doing things he never dreamed of doing before his conversion, like kissing a leper, completely identifying with the poor, and listening carefully for directions from the Lord. One day, he thought he heard

What is an "ecological footprint"? Answer: "A measure of how much of the Earth's carrying capacity it takes to sustain humanity's consumption of goods and services."

Presbyterians Today,
May 2007

God speaking to him, "Francis, go and repair my church which as you see is falling into ruins."[23] He began at once to repair an old church building.

Then on that eventful St. Matthias's Day, God revealed to him how he was going to repair the church—not so much by actually restoring old church buildings, but rather by renewing the inner spiritual life of the church. The gospel of the day spelled out for him the pattern to follow. Now he would be "this Happy Traveler" as contemporary Thomas of Celano called him. He would walk about his native land proclaiming the good news of the kingdom.

Soon Francis gathered three companions—Bernard, Peter Catrani, and Giles. Before long he had other recruits. They dressed in a simple habit shaped like a cross, with a hood, and a rope tied around the waist. Eventually, Francis wrote a simple rule, went to Rome, and received the approval of the powerful Pope Innocent III. The rule reflected the simple life Francis insisted upon for his followers, often called friars or the Brothers Minor. They accepted a life of poverty as they traveled around the countryside preaching the gospel always, sometimes with words.

Though Francis might have been included in the section on pilgrims and seekers, or in the section on prophets and social reformers, I chose to include him here with physicians and naturalists because no one ever had a greater appreciation for the natural world than Francis. He saw life as a whole and delighted in the beauty of God's creation, including not just human beings, but birds and animals, the sun and the moon, everything created by God. He might be considered the first Christian environmentalist. He had an extraordinary concern for God's universe. Francis was especially attracted to birds. He preached to them, and he seemed to have a calming effect upon them. He encouraged them to sing praises to their creator because they owed so much to God. He loved other animals too. Numerous stories are told of him helping animals in distress. In one such story, Francis tames a hungry wolf. Sometimes it is difficult to separate fact from legend, but there can be no doubt that Francis had a remarkable relationship with everything that lived. He even advocated that the authorities should designate Christmas Day as a date when everyone should feed the birds and the animals.

Shortly before his death, Francis composed a song, sometimes referred to as "The Canticle of the Sun," in which he called upon the whole creation to praise God. In this most personal song, Francis called on "brother sun," "sister moon," "brother wind," "sister water,"

With 105 million dogs in the United States, walkers might expect to trip over leashes on every street corner. But William Winter, D.V.M., of Minneapolis, Minnesota, estimates that only about a third of those pooches pound the sidewalks with their owners. The rest stay cooped up in backyards, houses, and apartments, getting out only to "do their duty" and shuffling back inside for some rest.

*Mark Bricklin, editor
Walking for Health*

"brother fire," and "our mother earth" to praise God. Undoubtedly the Psalms influenced him, in particular, Psalm 148. Today, many of us sing the hymn "All Creatures of Our God and King" based upon Francis' original canticle.

According to Donald Spoto in his *Reluctant Saint: The Life of Francis of Assisi,* when Francis died in 1226 after a prolonged and severe illness, those closest to him reported that "many birds, called larks, flew low above the roof of the house where he lay, wheeling in a circle and singing."[24]

As we confront serious environmental issues in our own day, we look to our children and youth who show the most concern to lead the older generation, and they can have no better role model than Francis of Assisi.

Thought to Ponder

What does Francis of Assisi have to teach us as we face monumental environmental challenges in the twenty-first century?

Prayer

Instill in me, O God, a sense of appreciation for your whole creation—the sun, the moon, the stars, animals, birds, and human beings alike. May I join everything and everyone you have made in praising you from the depths of my being. Amen.

NEVER LOOK DOWN

Dag Hammarskjöld (1905-1961)

My steps have held fast to your paths;
my feet have not slipped.

PSALM 17:5

Sven Stolpe, one of Dag Hammarskjöld's biographers, observed that when-ever Hammarskjöld had the opportunity he fled into the wilderness, to the mountains. We might even say he had a romantic attachment to the mountains. Like Francis of Assisi, Hammarskjöld would fit into a number of categories—politician, pilgrim, prophet—but because of his fascination with God's creation, and in particular his fervent mountain climbing, I have placed him with the naturalists.

Hammarskjöld's father and mother, steeped in Swedish Lutheranism, had a profound impact upon his childhood and later life. From his father, Hjalmar, who was prime minister of Sweden during World War I, he inher-ited a keen sense of duty. From his mother, Agnes, who was a strongly com-mitted Lutheran Christian, he received a warm, emotional, personal faith. She was a close friend of Nathan Söderblom, the theologian and Archbishop of Uppsala. Agnes and Nathan were born on the same day; they had so much in common they were often called "the twins."[25] Although Hammarskjöld's father seldom attended worship on Sunday, the son always went with his mother to church, not just as a boy but also later in his adulthood.

Hammarskjöld attended the universities of Uppsala and Stockholm, majoring in law and economics. Early in his career he was associated with the Bank of Sweden, but in 1946 he switched his interest to the foreign minis-try. By 1952, he had become chairman of Sweden's delegation to the United Nations and, in 1953, he was elected secretary-general. He died tragically in a 1961 airplane crash while seeking a cease-fire between the United Nations and Katanga forces in Africa.

After the airplane crash, a personal diary was found among his posses-sions. In 1965, the diary was published with the simple title *Markings*, includ-ing a forward by the poet W. H. Auden. In the light of the published diary, the world came to know another side of this highly visible dignitary

What has impressed me most of all about his spiritual diary is the pervasiveness of the walking image. For example, he described his overwhelming sense of God driving his life toward an ultimate purpose in the following words: "Never look down to test the ground before taking the next step: only he who keeps his eyes fixed on the far horizon will find the right road."[26] He inscribed these words while still in his twenties.

> *Mountains offer the slow unfolding of panoramas and the exhilaration of high places. Their summits, even the humble ones, are nearly always pinnacles of experience.*
>
> *Fletcher & Rawlins*
> The Complete Walker IV

Hammarskjöld kept company with Christian spiritual writers, and he explained his own quest with these words: "The longest journey is the journey inwards."[27] He was an introspective man who did not wear his piety on his sleeve, but reading and rereading his personal diary should convince almost anyone that his outer political activism was fueled by an inner journey of tremendous force. He felt at one with God's created world and once exclaimed, "In a dream I walked with God through the deep places of creation."[28]

He used his mountain climbing experiences to describe the risks of the life of faith: "Really, nothing was easier than to step from one rope ladder to the other—over the chasm. But, in your dream, you failed, because the thought occurred to you that you might possibly fall.[29]

Again, mountain climbing is compared to the perseverance required by the spiritual seeker: "When the morning's freshness has been replaced by the weariness of midday, when the leg muscles quiver under the strain, the climb seems endless, and, suddenly, nothing will go quite as you wish—it is then that you must *not* hesitate."[30]

Much as he loved the Christian mystics, Hammarskjöld was not a quietist who left everything to God, but rather affirmed, "In our era the road to holiness necessarily passes through the world of action."[31]

Did Hammarskjöld discern that death was near? In the spring of 1961, the year of the fatal airplane crash, he wrote in his diary:

> The gate opens: dazzled,
> I see the arena,
> Then I walk out naked
> To meet my death.[32]

From beginning to end, Dag Hammarskjöld did not look down but kept his eyes on the goal, the mission he believed God had given him. He was a phenomenal walker and mountain climber who really felt at home in the natural world, a singular combination of mystic and activist. He has given us an admirable example to emulate.

Thought to Ponder

Dag Hammarskjöld had his eyes fixed on the "far horizon" and his ultimate goal. What is the driving force of your own life that moves you forward to realize your dreams?

Prayer

Gracious God, I thank you that your call leads me onward and your strength keeps me from falling when I stumble along the way. Amen.

BASIC ITEMS FOR HIKERS:

1. Adequate food.
2. Extra clothing, including rain gear.
3. Pocket knife.
4. First aid kit.
5. Matches in a weatherproof container.
6. Sunglasses.
7. Compass.
8. Fire starting material.
9. Flashlight with extra batteries.
10. Map of the hike you plan and of the immediate area.

Philip Ferranti
Hiking

Rambling Late and Early

John James Audubon (1785-1851)

I know all the birds of the air,
and all that moves in the field is mine.

Psalm 50:11

A lice Ford has provided an excellent compilation of the writings of John James Audubon, pioneer birder and extraordinary artist. In one of his writings, Audubon describes his exploration of the American frontier as follows: "To study Nature was, to me, to ramble through their domains late and early."[33]

Audubon did ramble indeed, first as a teenager in his new American home just north of Philadelphia. Later, he would settle in Louisville, Kentucky, and roam the woods in that area. Still later, he sailed down the Ohio and Mississippi rivers and lived in the New Orleans area for a number of years. In the end, he found fame when he took his bird paintings to England, but he became homesick for America and his beloved woods.

Born out of wedlock in 1785 in the Caribbean, Audubon was the son of a French businessman and a young French chambermaid. His father sent him to the United States in 1803, when he was eighteen years old, to oversee the family property at Mill Grove on Perkiomen Creek, northwest of Philadelphia. An even more important reason for sending Audubon to the United States was his father's fear that John might be conscripted into Napoleon's army.

Audubon enjoyed his new surroundings. He soon learned to speak English, and before long in his rambles around the countryside he met Lucy Green Bakewell, who also loved walking long distances in the world of nature. They fell in love, but her family did not permit them to be married until 1808.

Audubon never showed much skill as an overseer of his father's property. Before long, he left for New York, where he learned the import-export trade in the firm where Lucy's brother Tom worked. At that time, much of New York was still rural, and Richard Rhodes, Audubon's recent biographer, notes that, "He could cross the

> *The many summers I took church groups to hike the Appalachian Trial are the closest experiences I have had to the fellowship of the first Christians that we read about in the book of Acts.*
>
> Tom P. Hafer
> Faith & Fitness

*The Wilderness Road
from Virginia through the
Cumberland Gap to the
Ohio Valley, opened by men
working on foot and first
traveled by pedestrians, was
the only existing route for
those wanting to cross the
Appalachian Mountains.
. . . Daniel Boone blazed
the original trail in 1775.*

Joseph A. Amato
On Foot

city of seventy-five thousand people in minutes at his characteristically swift, vigorous walk."[34]

Later, on the Illinois prairie, he walked the same way, prompting Rhodes to write, "Throughout his life Audubon would always be a phenomenal walker, on good roads managing even a series of eight-minute miles, walking as fast as many people run."[35]

After John and Lucy married they moved to Louisville, Kentucky, settling in the nearby town of Henderson. To support his family, Audubon operated a dry goods store, but he always found time to explore the woods in search of birds to paint and add to his collection. Although the store prospered for a time, he was forced into bankruptcy during the financial panic of 1819.

Starting life anew, John and Lucy left Kentucky and sailed down the Ohio and Mississippi Rivers to New Orleans. Audubon continued to paint local birds in the nearby woods while Lucy taught for wealthy plantation families and cared for their children. John especially enjoyed his Sundays exploring birds in the woods, except on those occasions when the river flooded and gushed over the levee.

In 1826, Audubon sailed for England with his collection of paintings. He arrived in Liverpool and spent much of his time walking the streets in search of a publisher, to no avail. The people did take notice, however, of this strange American and his swift walking gait.

Audubon loved the city of Edinburgh, but he detested London's shocking poverty and dense population. Nevertheless, the contacts he made in Edinburgh led him to a publisher in London who was willing to buy his bird collection, which was published as *Birds of America*.

During this period in England, Audubon missed his wife, Lucy. Letters were often delayed or lost at sea. Misunderstandings occurred between John and Lucy. Yearning to be home with his wife, John finally set sail for America and arrived in New York City in 1829. In his later life, Audubon traveled around the country seeking to complete a more thorough study of all the birds of America. He became a close friend of John Bachman, a Lutheran pastor in Charleston, South Carolina, who shared Audubon's passion for walking and birding. Bachman's two daughters would marry Audubon's two sons, and

Bachman and his two sons-in-law collaborated in preparing Audubon's final work, *Viviparous Quadrupeds of North America*, published in 1845. Audubon died on January 27, 1851, and was buried in Trinity Cemetery in New York City.

Underlying John Audubon's incomparable legacy of birding and caring for the natural environment was his ardent desire and practice, throughout his sixty-six years, "to ramble" in the woods, "late and early."

Thought to Ponder

John James Audubon had a craving to know "all the birds of the air" in God's creation, and he devoted his life to painting as many birds as he could see. Has a similar challenge to do something special for God gripped your own life? How have you pursued this summons?

Prayer

God of the universe, help me to see your grandeur everywhere. Give me an appreciation of birds, animals, the sky, and the sea—all of your spectacular creation. Though I may not have the gift of painting part of your creation, like the psalmist, may I honor you with sacrifices of thanksgiving. Amen.

ROGER'S ITCHY FEET

Roger Tory Peterson (1908-1996)

Lay aside immaturity, and live,
and walk in the way of insight.

PROVERBS 9:6

In 1975 Roger Tory Peterson was voted "the most famous person to have ever come out of Jamestown." (He won by one vote over actress Lucille Ball.) Nevertheless, Peterson thought it was quite an accomplishment for a mere naturalist.

The Jamestown in question is Jamestown, New York, just south of beautiful Chautauqua Lake, in the western part of the state. Peterson always seemed to love birds, but his seventh grade teacher really motivated him to do serious birding. She organized a Junior Audubon Club that emphasized field trips and not just book learning. Soon Peterson was out in the woods. He found time to watch birds, identify them, and then use his inherent artistic skill to make field sketches. Although slender of build, and not very athletic, his legs became strong through his many hours of walking.

After high school Peterson painted designs on furniture for a while. Even though his father saw no future for his son's interest in birds, Peterson left Jamestown and studied in New York City, first at the Arts Student League from 1927 to 1928, and then at the National Academy of Design from 1929 to 1931. Later, he became an instructor in science and art at the Rivers School in Brookline, Massachusetts. During this period in his life he began to make contact with other people expert in the world of bird watching, and he joined them in countless excursions into the countryside.

One such walk changed Peterson's life in a dramatic way. John C. Devlin and Grace Naismith, in *The World of Roger Tory Peterson*, explain what happened. Peterson had made friends with William Vogt, a nature columnist who knew birds well. Peterson and Vogt went out one December day in 1930, counting ducks along the Hudson River. Peterson's ability to identify birds by sight and hearing astounded Vogt. At length, he turned to the young man and said, "Roger, you know more

When you reach the top of a mountain that you spent the last hour hiking up, you might not hear birds, insects, wind, or any sound at all at first. Then God will speak.

Tom P. Hafer
Faith & Fitness

about identifying birds of this region than almost anyone else, and you can paint. Why don't you pass on your knowledge to other people in a book?"[36] They discussed the idea as they made their mile-long trek through the cattails back to their car. By that time, Vogt had convinced Peterson he should have a go at it.

Houghton Mifflin published Peterson's first book, *A Field Guide to the Birds*, in 1934. He was twenty-five years old. The publisher did not even pay royalties on the first one thousand copies; nevertheless, Peterson was elated. He had shown how birds might be identified by careful observation of specific markings on each bird. His brilliant paintings made each bird come alive. Earlier guide books assumed the reader had a dead bird in hand and could make observations and measurements. Peterson's method made it easy for the reader to quickly pick out the birds by specific field marks.

Peterson traveled all over the world in his remaining years, covering all seven continents. He walked and walked and kept perfecting his field guide. One friend likened him to the ancient Vikings for his love of travel and remarked about "Roger's itchy foot."[37] He continued his birding expeditions until he died at the grand age of eighty-seven.

Roger Peterson inspired millions of people to take up the hobby of bird watching, and his guidebooks indirectly roused these same people to get out and walk to accomplish their aim. As Jean Craighead George contends in *The American Walk Book*, "Perhaps the greatest boon to walking and the one that changed the character of the American walk was the advent of field guides, the little hip-pocket books for identifying birds, mammals, wildflowers, insects, trees, and minerals."[38]

Roger Tory Peterson's guidebooks led the way in this explosion of interest for walking in nature. "Roger's itchy foot" has been contagious, and not a few people have been infected by this sublime adventure.

Mennonite professor Arthur Paul Boers grew up thinking there were no interesting birds in his area: *Years later, when I lived in Indiana for the first time, I went for daily walks through a nearby park along a river. One day, for some reason, a friend loaned me a camera zoom lens and I took it with me. I used it to look more closely at trees, bushes, and the riverbank. My walk was a lot slower that day, and thereafter too, because I discovered a bird cornucopia that I had no idea existed.*

Arthur Paul Boers
The Rhythm of
God's Grace

Thought to Ponder

When his friend William Vogt suggested to young Roger Tory Peterson that he consider using his knowledge of birding to prepare a field guide for recognizing birds, Roger could not have realized he would be starting something that would have a salutary effect upon millions of people. Have friends suggested to you that you have interests and gifts God could use in a unique ministry? Ponder these suggestions.

Prayer

O God of the future, I thank you for friends. So often I do not see myself as other people see me. Could I be overlooking or discounting gifts I have that you could use to bless other people? Lord, may I not be immature but gain insight into my own potential from whatever source it may come. Amen.

POETS
&
NOVELISTS

The Wanderer

Johann Wolfgang Goethe (1749-1832)

When you walk, your step will not be hampered.

PROVERBS 4:12

Of all the creative walkers mentioned in this book, surely Goethe, the German genius, used the most bizarre way to overcome indecision in his youthful quest to ascertain his true vocation in life. Born in Frankfurt am Main, Germany, in 1749, he grew up in a wealthy family with all the cultural and educational benefits usually associated with such privilege. He studied law at Leipzig University for three years before his health failed him. Returning home, his health improved and he finished his law degree at the University of Strasbourg in 1771.

One day as he walked on the right bank of the Rhine River, Goethe wrestled with the decision of whether or not to be an artist. On impulse, he devised a daring stunt to settle the matter. He took a handsome pocketknife and threw it in the river. If the pocketknife fell into the water, he would become an artist.

What happened? He received no absolute answer. He could not see the pocketknife hit the water, but he thought he heard a splash of water. He interpreted this ambiguous sign to mean that he should not be a traditional artist. He would commit himself to painting the picture of the human condition with words.[1]

Goethe began writing poetry, plays, and novels. *The Sorrows of Young Werther,* written in 1774, brought him instant fame throughout Europe. The story told of a young man who, unable to control his passions, committed suicide. In 1775, Goethe moved to Weimar, his home for the rest of his life, although he traveled widely, not only within Germany, but also in Switzerland and Italy.

Philosopher Gottfried Herder's love of nature stimulated Goethe. Dramatist Friedrich Schiller shared long walks with Goethe and encouraged him to complete his masterpiece, *Faust,* a story that Goethe kept revising throughout most of his adult life. He and Schiller often

A walking tour in the city of Weimar, Germany invariably leads to the pedestrian area and the Theaterplatz featuring the Goethe-and-Schiller monument dedicated to the city's most famous residents.

"Excursion to Weimar"

walked on the road high above the Nectar River at Heidelberg, where they shared their thoughts and feelings along the *Philosophenweg,* or Philosophers' Way.

Like the biblical book of Job, *Faust* begins with God and the devil making a wager on Faust. God is certain Faust will remain faithful. The devil tempts Faust with the offer, "I will be your slave in this world, if you will consent to be my slave in the next."[2] Faust as a young man tastes all the sensual pleasures of the world, and yet he does not find real fulfillment. Upon further reflection he decides to poison himself and end it all, but, at the last moment, he hears an Easter hymn and decides to live. Henceforth, he engages in a variety of adventures, but still he is not satisfied. Finally, he decides to drain a swamp so that people can live in the area. He forgets himself, and he begins to think of others. Unfortunately, at the moment of his supreme happiness, the devil comes to claim his share. But then God's angels intervene and carry Faust to heaven because he has learned to strive for others rather than for himself. This greatest of all Goethe's work was completed a few months before his death.

Goethe's other literary works included love and nature poems, and numerous novels that made him, in his later years, the most celebrated author in Europe. His autobiography, *Poetry and Truth,* was published between 1811 and 1814, but the last part did not appear until 1833, after he died.

Nicholas Boyle, in his careful study of Goethe's life, notes that Goethe derived inspiration for his writing from his love of the outdoors, and in particular, from his long, energetic walks along the Rhine River, as well as from his strenuous mountain climbing. The Swiss Alps had a special attraction to him. He was thrilled with the landscape of the Bernese Oberland and the Pennine Alps. He rejoiced in high-altitude hiking as he made his way over the famed St. Gotthard Pass on his way to Italy. The outings in the mountains were not just pleasure trips to him—they were also a conscious literary exercise. Everything he observed in the landscape became what he called "the material of poetry."[3]

Early in his life Goethe's friends dubbed him "The Wanderer,"[4] because it was not uncommon for him to make seventeen-mile hikes in one day. Long walks and

A friend of mine told me about seeing a bumper sticker that read: "All who wander are not lost." When we find ourselves on the road again, it doesn't mean we are lost. We believe that our wandering is watched over by the One who is its initiator.

Sara Covin Juengst
The Road Home

vigorous mountain climbing combined to spark fire in Goethe's writing to the end of his days, but his sense of vocation was formed that day on the path above the Rhine River when in an impromptu manner he vowed to be a writer—and what a creative writer he became!

Thought to Ponder

What do you think of Goethe's bizarre way of deciding his future vocation? Can you think of better ways, with a biblical basis, to determine what God's call might be for your life? Proverbs 4:12 has a promise for us.

Prayer

Lord, help me to pray and listen to your voice in the scriptures as I seek to know what vocation I should pursue in life. Amen.

I WALKED WITH MY BROTHER AT MY SIDE

William Wordsworth (1770-1850)
Dorothy Wordsworth (1771-1855)

Do two walk together
unless they have an appointment?

AMOS 3:3

There is a yarn often told about William Wordsworth that when a visitor asked to see the famous poet's study, Wordsworth's housekeeper said that his library was in the house but his study was the great out-of-doors. William Wordsworth yearned to be a major English poet. He had his share of dry periods and also his moments of extraordinary inspiration. Some scholars rank him among the very best of the Romantic poets.

Wordsworth once defined poetry as "emotion recollected in tranquility." Invariably, it was after an extensive walking tour by himself, or more likely with his sister Dorothy or other close friends such as Samuel Taylor Coleridge, that William would be animated as he reflected "in tranquility" about the excitement of the day. More often than not, William and Dorothy ambled in their favorite Lake District in England, although they both also took extended expeditions around the rest of England and on the Continent.

The singular walk that gave Wordsworth a lifelong passion for hiking in the world of nature was his grand tour of Europe in 1770. When his term ended at Cambridge University, he walked no less than 350 miles in two weeks throughout France, Switzerland and Italy. Before his life ended he walked an estimated 175,000 miles.

Something is wrong with a society in which a pedestrian runs more risk of injury than persons in any motorized transportation, including motorcycling.

Leonard Sweet
The Jesus Prescription
for a Healthy Life

While in France he was caught up in the fervor of the French Revolution. Returning to England, he gave support to liberal political and social action. Later in life, however, he toned down his political and social zeal, and, indeed, became quite conservative.

After his return to England, Wordsworth began writing seriously and collaborated with Coleridge in producing the popular *Lyrical Ballads* in 1798. He began to

write his major work, *Prelude*, in 1798, and he continued to revise it throughout the rest of his life.

Wordsworth had a unique relationship with his
sister Dorothy, who also had a keen appreciation for
poetry. She loved, adored, and idolized her brother. No
two siblings were ever closer. Above all, she and William were intense walkers, trekking thousands of miles
together in England and on the Continent.

Dorothy was born in 1771, a year after her brother.
They lived in Cockermouth, a small town in the northern end of England's captivating Lake District. Tragedy
struck their peaceful home in 1778, when their mother,
Ann, came down with pneumonia and died. The family
separated. Dorothy had to live with her mother's cousin
in Halifax. She would not see William for nine years.

> *When Jesus called Peter to*
> *come to him across the water,*
> *Peter, for one brief, glorious*
> *moment, remembered how,*
> *and strode with ease across*
> *the lake. This is how we are*
> *meant to be, and then we*
> *forget, and we sink. But if*
> *we cry out for help (as Peter*
> *did) we will be pulled out of*
> *the water, we won't drown.*
> *And if we listen, we will*
> *hear, and if we look, we*
> *will see.*
>
> *Madeleine L'Engle*
> Walking on Water

In 1787, Dorothy returned from Halifax to Penrith,
where William lived with their grandparents. By the time she was reunited
with her brother, she was a grown woman of nearly sixteen. In a short time,
William was off to Cambridge. During this interlude Dorothy wrote faithfully to him. In William's poem *An Evening Walk*, he recalled the sights and
sounds of his home country. The tone of the poem makes one suspect he was
writing to his cherished walking companion, Dorothy.

In 1794, William and Dorothy bought a farmhouse in Windy Brow, on
the hillside above Keswick. Dorothy was delighted to be with her brother
again and kept house for him. William, too, was deeply satisfied being with
Dorothy and enjoyed walking the countryside with her. Later, they moved
to other locations, finally settling in Grasmere, where they lived together for
eight years. Even when William married Mary Hutchinson and they raised a
family of their own, Dorothy lived in the same house.

William and Dorothy took many walking tours together. They traveled
with Coleridge to Germany in 1798, but they both were sick on the voy-
age and the dirt and filth of the city of Hamburg repelled them. Later, William decided to take Dorothy with him as he revisited Wales, where he had
tramped with Robert Jones in an earlier time. They undertook a four-day
ramble that eventually brought them to the ruins of Tintern Abbey beside the
River Wye. The abbey's ivy-clad stone shell stirred William's imagination, and
he later wrote one of his most memorable poems, *Lines Composed a Few Miles
above Tintern Abbey*, based upon this visit.

Wordsworth, writing in *Prelude*, explained how walking undisturbed
through the natural world helped him to probe the deep mystery of the
human soul:

Happy in this, that I with nature walked,
Not having a too early intercourse
With the deformity of crowded life.[5]

Dorothy's thrill of walking with her brother is best summed up in an excerpt from one of her letters: "I walked with my brother at my side, from Kendal to Grasmere, eighteen miles, and afterwards from Grasmere to Keswick, fifteen miles, through the most delightful country that ever was seen."[6]

This phenomenal brother and sister team motivated each other to write verse that continues to speak to the human condition even today.

Thought to Ponder

Contemplating the unique relationship of William and Dorothy Wordsworth, and their ardor as walking companions, have you known or observed others in their walk with God who have nourished and been nourished by one another?

Prayer

Gracious God, as I walk with you in my own spiritual journey, may I be conscious of other pilgrims along the way who may need my help, and who may also be of help to me when I falter. Amen.

The Deep Woods—Coolness

Wallace Stevens (1879-1955)

They heard the sound of the LORD God
walking in the garden at the time
of the evening breeze.

GENESIS 3:8

Annie Dillard, in *The Writing Life,* describes Wallace Stevens's typical day as an insurance executive living in Hartford, Connecticut, during his forties:

> He rose at six, read for two hours, and walked another hour—three miles to work. He dictated poems to his secretary. He ate no lunch at noon; he walked for another hour, often to an art gallery. He walked home from work—another hour. After dinner he retired to his study; he went to bed at nine. On Sundays he walked in the park.[7]

There is no question that walking played a large part in this unusual man's life, a man who combined poetry with his day job in the insurance industry. He continued walking throughout his adult life until he injured his ankle in a fall during the winter season. He never fully recovered from this accident.

Born in Reading, Pennsylvania, he was married in the First Presbyterian Church of that city. He later moved to Hartford. Although a brilliant writer of poetry, his published work is often difficult to read. He saw the universe in dark colors with much distress and despondency, but he also saw signs of hope as well for those people who could use their imagination. He tended to identify the divine with imagination, and he was convinced the riddle of the universe could only be understood through imagination.

Stevens's well-known poems include *Sunday Morning,* published in 1915; *The Emperor of Ice Cream,* 1922; and *The Idea of Order at Key West,* 1934. He also wrote a larger work, *Notes Toward a Supreme Fiction,* in 1942.

Stevens's *Collected Poems,* published in 1954, won the 1955 Pulitzer Prize. In his poem *Of the Surface of Things,* we observe the theme of walking:

> *Walking is an essential discipline of thought and spirit. My soul is a traveler afoot in the world. Like Aristotle (whose school was called Peripatetic, after the covered walkway along which he strolled while teaching), I cannot think clearly if I remain too long sedentary.*
>
> Sam Keen
> Hymns to an
> Unknown God

In my room the world is beyond my understanding,
But when I walk I see that it consists of three or four hills and a
cloud.[8]

Despite Stevens's sharp mind, he had a great fear of appearing in public.
He went through intense preparation himself to speak to large audiences.
In a letter to Barbara Church, he comments upon his nervousness and tells
her how he attempts to combat his fears. He confesses, "If I can walk a few
hours beforehand and make myself tired, this almost completely eliminates
nerves."[9]

Although Stevens enjoyed traveling on foot almost anywhere, he did have
a favorite place that always gave him a sense of calmness in facing his fears.
Elizabeth Park in Hartford, noted for its beautiful rose gardens, was the ideal
spot for his leisurely strolls. This regular practice enabled him to pull himself together to meet other people. He returned to Elizabeth Park again and
again.

In another letter to Barbara Church, he comments upon the bad weather
in this particular springtime, but he does notice that the crocuses are up and
the robins are beginning to return. He then writes of the birdsong he antici-
pates: "It is such a joy to hear them in the early morning and again in the
evening as I walk home, even though, so far away from the mating season,
they are nothing to what they will be then."[10]

In still another letter to Church, he exclaims, "I walked in the little park
near us, before starting to town this morning. There
is good enough woods there and I inhaled the deep
woods–coolness."[11]

That was Stevens's secret for overcoming his fear of
the public at large. He simply would stride alone amid
the flowers and the trees inhaling "the deep woods–coolness." Then he was ready for any challenge that would
come his way.

*Kenneth Cooper, M.D.,
who coined the term
"aerobics" once wrote: "I
think people should walk
more and run less."*

Casey Meyers
Walking

Thought to Ponder

We all need a quiet place to be alone with God so that we can absorb God's renewing presence and be fortified to overcome our weaknesses. Where is that quiet place for you?

Prayer

Comforting God, I know that I need a quiet center where I can withdraw from the heat of the day for a few moments and simply open up to the cool breezes of your Spirit. If Jesus needed to come apart from the crowds and pray, how much more do I. Thank you for the gift of solitude. Amen.

THE ROAD NOT TAKEN

Robert Frost (1874-1963)

I will instruct you and teach you
the way you should go;
I will counsel you with my eye upon you.

PSALM 32:8

New England poet Robert Frost is beloved for many popular poems, including *Birches, Mending Wall,* and *Stopping by Woods on a Snowy Evening.* Although born in San Francisco, his family moved backed to their original home in New England when Robert was about eleven years old. He attended Dartmouth and Harvard colleges, but he did not graduate from either one. He worked as a farmer and a schoolteacher before moving to England in 1912, where his poetry was received with wild acclaim.

After a few years, Frost returned to New England, where he continued to write poetry, most of which centered on New England scenes. He taught for a number of years at Amherst College, and he was a popular speaker on the college circuit. He won the Pulitzer Prize several times for his poetry. His career climaxed on a cold, windy day when he read his poetry at John F. Kennedy's inauguration as president of the United States.

A spirited walker all his life, Frost included walking as a theme in many of his poems. He often went with friends on long hikes, what he liked to call "botanizing walks." He tramped through the New England hills he knew so well, but he ambled other places too. When he thought his beloved Elinor no longer loved him and would not marry him, he fled to the Dismal Swamp, a frightening stretch of land along the Virginia-North Carolina border. He slogged through this barren land hoping to forget his rejection.

In 1922, Frost attempted an ambitious hike on the Long Trail extending from Bennington, Vermont, through the Green Mountains to the Canadian border. At Pico Peak, Frost developed problems with his feet and had to drop out. Biographer Jay Parini explains Frost's reaction: "I did something like 200 miles, most of them painful to the feet but all beautiful to the eye and

Imagine the surprise of frontiersman Daniel Boone when he was asked if he had ever been lost. "No," he replied slyly, "But I was bewildered once for three days."

Phil Cousineau
The Art of Pilgrimage

mind."[12] He would not quit hiking because he claimed such regular movement "stilled the mind" in a way that had a positive effect upon his poetry.

Of all his poems, the walking theme is most prominent in *The Road Not Taken*. There is some confusion about the exact influences that led to the writing of this well-known poem. One distinct influence was Edward Thomas, Frost's best friend during his stay in England. Frost recognized the poetic spirit within this man, and they often took long strolls through the English countryside. Frost noted, however, that Thomas frequently castigated himself for decisions he had made; in particular, for not taking some other path than the one he did. Later, when Frost wrote the poem and sent a copy to Thomas, his friend unfortunately failed to see himself in the poem.

Once warm weather returned, Rousseau's spirits rose, as they always did, and he resumed his wanderings in the hills. It happened that Du Peyrou was an enthusiastic amateur botanist, and under his influence Rousseau began to take a serious interest in an avocation that had bored him back in Chambéry.

Leo Damrosch
Jean-Jacques Rousseau: Restless Genius

Frost may have revealed another intriguing influence for *The Road Not Taken* in a letter he wrote to Susan Ward, dated February 10, 1912, shortly before he left for England. He describes in the letter what he experienced one day while walking in the winter woods. He came to a lonely crossroad and saw a Poe-like figure approaching someone who looked eerily like himself. In the poem Frost writes:

> Two roads diverged into a wood, and I—
> I took the one less traveled by,
> And that has made all the difference.[13]

Could it have been mere happenstance, asks biographer Jean Gould, "that Robert and his wife Elinor decided to leave Plymouth and seek a better 'climate' for poetry writing in England just after Robert had this mystical experience in the woods?"[14]

Parini, who sees the influence of his friend Edward Thomas as extremely significant, nevertheless comments that, "The overpowering simplicity of the image is archetypal in its appeal: every reader has stood at some fork and wondered which might be the better path. Most will have wanted to take 'the one less traveled by' and thus be a maverick or 'long striker.'"[15]

Whatever Frost's dominant motivation for writing *The Road Not Taken,* there can be no doubt that walking was a life-time passion of this New England poet and that the theme of walking permeated his poetry. Furthermore, this single poem has challenged many people to be daring at life's turning points.

Thought to Ponder

Have you missed some path you wish you had taken at an earlier time? Perhaps you did not have the time or the money to pursue your objective, but now the way may still be open. What unfulfilled dreams do you want to pursue? Do you have the courage to try the road not taken?

Prayer

Mighty God, grant me the courage to be adventurous in my spiritual journey and to not always be content with traveling the safe and easy course. Amen.

RAMBLE ON THE YORKSHIRE MOORS

Emily Brontë (1818-1848)

. . . how you followed me in the wilderness,
in a land not sown.

JEREMIAH 2:2

Most people might not think the lonely, bleak moors in northern England's Yorkshire region would be a place that would prompt creative writing, but for Emily Brontë, her rambles on the Yorkshire moors stimulated her imagination as no other environment.

Emily grew up in a poor parson's home in the dreary town of Haworth, a few miles beyond Keighley in Yorkshire. Her Irish-born father, Patrick Brontë, was influenced by the Evangelical Revival but he remained in the Church of England. His wife died, leaving him with six children. Two of them died very young, but his son Branwell grew to manhood. Three daughters—Charlotte, Emily, and Anne—also survived and each became a well-known novelist. Ironically, though sickly much of his life, the father outlived all of his children.

Emily was a very private person. Tall and angular, she often went for long spells without eating very much. She lived in a dream world she called *Gondal*, and many of her early poems came from this imaginary setting. Her younger sister Anne also shared in the fantasy world of Gondal. Emily left home for a time to be a governess, a position that involved not only providing for the material needs of the children under her care but also the responsibility of teaching them the rudiments of education. She had no formal training for such a task, and soon suffered a physical and emotional breakdown.

Returning home, she took care of her ailing father who was going blind and she watched over her irresponsible brother Branwell who was wasting his life away drinking, carousing, and doing drugs. She never knew

What do you do when urban development has destroyed walking and biking trails in your Bronx neighborhood? Majora Carter, 40, decided to do something about it. She led a protest against plans to develop a waste plant. In the end, she helped raise $30 million to bring walking paths back to her community.

Prevention Magazine

when Branwell would be coming home at night. Emily would go about her household chores while at the same time conjugating French and German verbs to expand her knowledge.

Emily's eccentric father had a habit each morning of rousing his family by taking a loaded pistol outside and firing a shot into the church tower. As it became increasingly difficult for him to see, he taught Emily to fire the pistol toward the now pock-filled tower. He probably trained Emily because he feared hitting one of his parishioners by accident one day.

What motivated Emily to write? She had innate ability and from an early age she wrote poetry and then later fiction, usually at night when others had gone to bed. Of course, being with her sisters, who also were gifted writers, awakened her own desires. Charlotte published *Jane Eyre,* Anne published *Agnes Grey,* and Emily published *Wuthering Heights,* all in the year 1847. Incidentally, the critics severely condemned Emily's book for its violence and its lack of traditional ethics.

Surely among the strongest encouragements Emily had for writing were her long walks on the moors that surrounded her home. Katherine Frank, in her biography of Emily, tells the story of how when she was only six years old she went out on the moors one day with her brother Branwell, sister Anne, and the servant Tabby. Suddenly a fierce storm arose, and the Crow Hill bog exploded, spewing peat, soil, and boulder down into the valley. Nonetheless, young Emily became excited with the beauty and violence erupting around her. Such an experience would not prevent her from returning again and again to her beloved moors.

Much of what we know about Emily comes through her sister Charlotte, who contended that, "Emily was passionately attached to the moors around her home, and spent a great deal of her solitude in their familiar embrace; away from the moors, Emily pined."[16]

Further testimony comes from John Greenwood, the village stationer, who provided the Brontës with writing materials. He kept a diary and one day he inscribed in his journal that he noticed Emily coming from one of her long walks on the moors, her cheeks flushed with exhilaration. As she greeted him that day, it seemed to him that "her countenance was lit with divine light."[17]

Biographer Frank sums up the influence of the moors as a singular incitement to Emily's writing: "Emily knew the landscape the way others know every

After Martin Luther's death some of his students collected and classified no less than 6,596 of the Reformer's sayings shared with others in informal settings and had them published in a volume entitled Table Talk. One of these sayings gives us insight into Luther's continual quest for truth: "They are trying to make me a fixed star. I am an irregular planet."

Roland Bainton
Here I Stand: A Life
of Martin Luther

mood and expression and tone of voice of a lover—intimately, deeply, in every season and in all weathers."[18]

A ramble through the Yorkshire moors was the tonic Emily needed to bolster her independent spirit. She would walk wherever nature led her; she had no need of any other guide.

Thought to Ponder

We all probably have been in a situation that at first seemed to be unpromising, but in the end became a place where God's creative energy was unleashed in us. Describe such a personal episode or an incident you know of.

Prayer

Lord, so many creative people have had their imagination stirred in the most unlikely places. Grant to me a consistency in my walking regimen that I may be ready to hear your Word speaking to me and showing me things I never dreamed possible. Amen.

A Long Walk in the Noisy Streets

Charles Dickens (1812-1870)

*I was in prison
and you visited me.*

MATTHEW 25:36

Charles Dickens has given us some of the most memorable characters in the literature of the English-speaking world. They include Tiny Tim and Ebenezer Scrooge in *A Christmas Carol,* Oliver in *Oliver Twist,* Mr. Micawber in *David Copperfield,* Sydney Carton in *The Tale of Two Cities,* Pip in *Great Expectations,* and Little Nell in *The Old Curiosity Shop,* to name just a few.

Dickens was a remarkable observer of human nature. He knew the people of his day and he could create unforgettable scenes, especially scenes featuring the downtrodden masses in the London slums. He identified with the poor and the oppressed and he attacked the rich and the powerful. When he was fifteen he quit school. In a short time he became a newspaper reporter, a job that further sharpened his powers of observation. Still in his early twenties, he published *The Pickwick Papers,* which became a sensation. In these papers, he depicted a group of eccentric characters involved in a series of humorous adventures.

Walking became an integral part of Dickens's preparation for writing. He walked everywhere. As he explained, "I am both a town traveler and a country traveler, and I am always on the road.[19]

In his early years, Dickens walked to release his enormous energy; his "daily constitutionals" as he called them became an obsession with him. He equated time spent walking with the time he spent writing. To him, traveling on foot was a "moral obligation." Although other men and women of his era were hearty walkers, what set Dickens apart was the fast pace he maintained. Most people could not keep up, such was his tremendous physical stamina. His brother-in-law exclaimed, "He looked the personification of energy, which seemed to ooze from every pore as from some hidden reser-

> *Whenever I walk somewhere, I try to walk quickly—at the age of seventy-four I don't walk as quickly as I once did, but more quickly than most people. I believe this improves my body, probably lengthens my life, and makes me slightly more alert.*
>
> Paul Simon
> Fifty-Two Simple Ways
> to Make a Difference

voir."[20] Later in life, Dickens went on foot as a means to ward off melancholy. By that time, he had many worries to keep him occupied.

When Dickens traveled outside England, he spent much of his time hiking around the new terrain. Even the Swiss marveled at his ability to tramp in the majestic Alps. His biographer, Peter Ackroyd, comments, "Dickens was so agile and nimble in his climbing that the Swiss guides nicknamed him 'The Intrepid'. . . and this was the scenery he loved—the precipices, the abysses beneath his feet, the narrow ledges, the rocks, all making up a picture of 'general desolation.'"[21]

The greatest distance ever walked nonstop is 234 miles by Britain's Thomas Benson. He covered the distance around the Aintree Race Course in 1978. It took him four days and four nights.

John Man
Walk!

In Dickens's trip to America, his athletic skills set him apart from others. He commented, "I am respected for my activity, inasmuch as I jump from the boat to the towing-path, and walk five or six miles before breakfast."[22]

But of all Dickens's perambulation, what he loved best was to walk in the busy streets, principally at night. One of his daughters explained, "A long walk in the noisy streets would act upon him as a tonic."[23] He could not seem to write unless he was immersed in the London crowds. They did something to him that nothing else could do. They were a "magic lantern" to him that made his writing come alive.

Dickens's nocturnal wanderings found vivid expression in "Night Walkings" recorded in *All the Year Round.* Another biographer, Brian Murray, understood Dickens's habit of walking at night through the city as a way to connect with the poor: "As a result of these wanderings Dickens—aiming 'to get through the night'—found also that the state of 'houselessness' brought him into sympathetic relations with people who have no other object every night of the year."[24]

Dickens's extraordinary characters were formulated in his mind as he ambled through London's "noisy streets" at night. As he walked past the prisons he heard the cries of the inmates. He could feel their pain. These long nocturnal walks, he always contended, animated him to write so colorfully and so poignantly about people who hurt.

Thought to Ponder

If London's noisy nighttime streets could be used by Dickens to create poignant novels about forgotten people who had genuine worth as human beings, where might you find such inspiration to share the good news of the gospel?

Prayer

Compassionate God, help me to identify completely with the people I seek to help, and not try to serve them at arm's length with a detached coldness. As I reach out to "the least of these" you have promised I will meet my Lord face to face. Amen.

WALKING THE CITY WITH A PURPOSE

Jorge Luis Borges (1899-1986)

Wisdom cries out in the street;
in the squares she raises her voice.
At the busiest corner she cries out;
at the entrance of the city gates she speaks.

PROVERBS 1:20-21

Jorge Luis Borges, a native of Argentina and a man of wide philosophical and cultural tastes, was an extraordinary poet, essayist, and a master of the short story. Like many other creative writers, he was a diligent walker who went on long walks when fresh ideas failed to emerge in his writing.

Borges grew up in the northern Buenos Aires neighborhood of Palermo, an area that was run-down in his day. His middle-class family, who spoke Spanish and English fluently, did not seem to fit into this environment, and yet many of Borges's short stories had their basis in his old neighborhood. In fact, the young Borges would tramp endlessly through the streets taking in the sights and sounds with astute appreciation.

Borges's father, who eventually became blind (as did Jorge), was a lawyer and a teacher with an ambition to be a writer; however, he had only one of his novels published. Jorge's mother came from a distinguished family of freedom fighters.

In 1914, the Borges family moved to Geneva, Switzerland, where they lived for four years while Jorge's father sought medical treatment for his failing eyesight. Jorge studied at the School of Geneva, founded by the Protestant reformer John Calvin. During his first stay in Geneva, Borges did not like the city, but later he would change his mind and enjoy this beautiful city so much that he desired to be buried there. In Geneva, he first thought of becoming a writer. He spent much time with two young Jewish friends—Maurice Abramowicz and Simon Jichlinski—and they stayed out late at night wandering the streets of Geneva "discussing everything and nothing."

In 1926, his family having returned to Argentina, Borges determined to do for Buenos Aires what James Joyce did for Dublin, Ireland; namely, he wanted to mythologize Buenos Aires. Evaristo Carriego, an Argentine poet, influenced Jorge at this juncture of his life. What Borges attempted to do was

to find the soul of the city in the poor barrios. His epic work would honor the everyday life of ordinary people in the great metropolis.

To accomplish his objective, Borges gathered around himself poets and writers to stimulate his own thinking. Biographer Edwin Williamson comments, "Borges was their leader, and, having always been fond of taking long walks, he now urged his friends to walk the city with a purpose—to 'feel Buenos Aires, to familiarize themselves with the different barrios and imbibe firsthand the stories, songs, and legends of the common people.'"[25] This concentrated effort resulted in Borges's major work, *The Aleph*, in which he sought to transform his early experiences in the barrios into a universal myth.

In 1946, Juan Peron became president of Argentina, and before long Borges wrote critical essays challenging his dictatorial powers. Borges espoused democratic ideals, yet one of his political contradictions was his fear that the masses would choose unwisely. In the end, he became disillusioned with most governments. He became a pacifist and claimed that the Swiss confederations constituted the ideal government.

With each passing decade, Borges's writings became better known beyond his native Argentina, but it was not until the 1960s that he gained world recognition. In 1961 he shared with Samuel Beckett the International Publishers Prize. Soon his works found publication in English and he received countless invitations to lecture in the United States.

Old Palermo in Buenos Aires: "It used to be a hangout for petty thieves and other people of doubtful character, but also a refuge for poets of the stature of Evaristo Carriego and Jorge Luis Borges, as well as a place where the tango of that time survived in this bohemian milieu. Today, it is an area of small restaurants and interesting antique shops, somewhere to spend an afternoon or nights in, when the light of streetlamps make the shadows come alive and cast a peculiar and attractive light over the scene."

www.enjoy-argentina.org

In 1967, Borges married Elsa Astete Millan, but the marriage lasted less than three years. In the last two decades of his life, he developed a romantic relationship with Maria Kodama, one of his students. Maria's father was Japanese and her mother was an Argentine. Maria, a constant companion to the now blind Borges, married him during the last year of his life. Although Borges traveled all over the world in the last three decades of his life, he always relished the opportunity to show guests his boyhood neighborhood in Buenos Aires. Despite his blindness, he still knew every inch of the beloved barrios that had inspired so much of his writing. He walked and talked with his guests, and he would proudly exclaim, "These places mean a great deal to me; they are my past."[26]

While Borges lived in Geneva at the close of his days, a dispute arose in Argentina over the sale of his house. What belonged to him and what belonged to other members of the family? Finally, matters were settled, and it turned out what indisputably belonged to Jorge were his books, his awards, and, of course, "his walking sticks."[27]

Jorge Luis Borges died on June 14, 1986, in Geneva. He called himself an "agnostic mystic" and "a weaver of dreams," but on his deathbed he welcomed a Roman Catholic priest and a Protestant pastor. His funeral was held in the Protestant Cathedral of Saint Peter and he was buried in the official cemetery, not far from John Calvin's grave.

Thought to Ponder

Is your own walking preference to aimlessly walk to and fro or, like Borges, are you walking for a purpose? If the latter, what is that clear-cut purpose?

Prayer

Merciful God, I give you thanks for the place where I live. I do not wish to live somewhere else. Help me to see the enormous potential of this place for serving you and others around me. Amen.

Once you're over the hill, you pick up speed.
Charles M. Schulz
Around the World in 45 Years

The Long Walk

James Michener (1907-1997)

. . . he has gone on a long journey.

PROVERBS 7:19

One of James Michener's critics once quipped when asked about Michener's soon-to-be published book: "My best advice is don't read it, my second best is don't drop it on your foot."[28]

Michener did write a number of big books, and most of them were bestsellers. Even though the critics might not like his literary style, the general public does. His first work of fiction was a collection of stories based upon his World War II experiences entitled *Tales of the South Pacific*, published in 1947. This first book won him the Pulitzer Prize for fiction in 1948. A year later Richard Rodgers and Oscar Hammerstein used the book as the basis for their hugely successful musical comedy *South Pacific*.

Among Michener's big novels were: *Sayonara, Hawaii, The Source, Centennial, Chesapeake, The Covenant, Texas, Alaska,* and *Caribbean*. Michener did not claim to be a great writer, but he did say he was the best "re-writer." Like Henry David Thoreau, Michener saw a direct relationship between the quality of his writing and the length of his daily walks.

Born in New York City, Michener grew up in the small hamlet of Doylestown in Bucks County, Pennsylvania, not far from the Delaware River. He walked daily and continued doing so well into his eighties whether he was at home or away on one of his many trips.

What was the seminal period in his life when he began to take walking seriously? Michener states it was while he was still a young man studying in Scotland. He was emboldened by other Scottish hikers. One day he accepted a challenge to trek across the breadth of the whole country. In his autobiography, *The World Is My Home*, he remarks: "Twice I walked completely across Scotland in two unbroken days, the first time covering nonstop a stretch of some sixty miles from St. Andrews toward Oban."[29]

He describes the second forty-eight mile trip in some detail. Leaving Inverness in the north, he trudged

The oldest track gold medalist was Tebbs Lloyd Johnson of Great Britain who was 48 when he walked off with the 1952 gold in the 3500m walk, the only time that event was held.

Nelson and MacNee
The Olympic Factbook

westward along its loch, then proceeding to Glen Affric and, through the pass between Ben Attow and Scour Ouran, he came down the western slopes to Invershiel. He never forgot this trip and claimed it was, "the kind of thing a man should do when young, and one of the most rewarding things about it was that I did it alone, so that the full force of nature could impress me and give me strength as I hiked through the dark hours."[30]

In Michener's book *Sports in America,* he elaborates and explains why this particular venture was so important to him: "It was this long walk that committed me to constant hiking, and . . . whenever I have been at home, I have left my desk almost every afternoon to walk with our dogs through the woods that surround the small plot of ground on which we live."[31]

Michener strolled every day except during blizzards and cloudbursts. He usually covered two or three miles in each trip through the fields and the woods. He never tired of his perambulating regimen. He was absolutely sure that there was a definite connection between his writing and his traveling on foot. In his own words, "When my writing goes poorly it is always because I have not walked enough, for it is on one of these uneventful and repetitious walks that I do my best thinking."[32]

In Michener's evening promenades he not only maintained physical fitness, but he contemplated his plots and developed his characters—thoughts, ideas, and insights to be written down the next morning at his writing desk. This practice, which he adhered to throughout most of his adult life well into his eighties, had its start and impetus when as a young man "the long walk" animated him to continue his "quiet rambles" for a lifetime.

Thought to Ponder

Call to mind a particular walk that had a transforming quality about it and started you on your way to physical, mental, or spiritual fitness. Share your elation with someone else.

Prayer

Eternal God, keep me alert to those special moments in my life when you are about to do something new. May such transforming moments lead to lifelong habits that will strengthen and invigorate me in serving other people. Amen.

Walking: "This is one of the most unheralded of Olympic track events. A women's 10k (10,000m) walk was added to the Olympic program in 1992. The walking race makes for an unusual spectacle as well, with men and women sashaying down the street, seemingly half-walking and half-running, shoulders pumping and hips rolling."

Nelson and MacNee
The Olympic Factbook

Steady Walks Free from Clocks

Robert Louis Stevenson (1850-1894)

I shall walk at liberty,
for I have sought your precepts.

Psalm 119:45

Robert Louis Stevenson took delight in shocking his business associates by appearing frequently at the office dressed in his hiking attire rather than a proper business suit. He usually walked to work and hiked for many miles on his free days. All he asked for was "the heaven above and the road below me."[33]

Stevenson, born in Edinburgh, Scotland, in 1850, had bad health from his childhood into adulthood. His weak lungs developed tuberculosis in his later years. At the age of seventeen he entered Edinburgh University to study engineering and later law, but his real love was reading and writing. He passed the bar examination, but he never practiced law.

To strengthen his weak lungs and poor health in general, he walked long distances. Eschewing the damp climate of Scotland, he traveled not only throughout Europe but also the United States. He married an American, Frances Osbourne, and they traveled together, eventually settling in the South Sea Islands in the Pacific Ocean. Stevenson died in 1894 on the island of Samoa.

In the course of wide travels, Stevenson's keen observations gave him rich material for his novels, short stories, poems, and other perceptive literature. Among his most popular works are *Treasure Island, Kidnapped, The Strange Case of Dr. Jekyll and Mr. Hyde*, and his enduring children's poem, *A Child's Garden of Verses*. In Stevenson's numerous letters, he often cites what walking meant to renewing his body, mind, and spirit. In a letter to Charles Baxter in 1872 he wrote, "I have been walking today by a colonnade of beeches along the brawling Allan. . . . I hold that he is a poor mean devil who can walk along, in such a place and in such weather, and doesn't set his lungs and cry back to the river.

> *[In 2002] a casual decision unexpectedly changed my life. I had resolved to use days off to hike the Bruce Trail, a 500-mile route following the Niagara Escarpment in southern Ontario. I did so even though I have never been athletic or outdoorsy. . . .*
> *I thought I was taking on a temporary challenge; instead, the Bruce Trail converted me.*
>
> *Arthur Paul Boers*
> The Christian Century

Follow, follow, follow me."[34] In a briefer comment, he told Sidney Colvin in an 1876 letter, "I am fit as a fiddle after my walk."[35]

To get an even clearer picture of what the peripatetic life meant to Stevenson, we may turn to his essay "Walking Tours." In this work he cannot hide his enthusiasm for going on foot. He is not sure which is greater—the anticipation of the journey or its completion. Everything about walking appealed to him. One pleasure leads to another pleasure.

He is quite emphatic that walking is best done alone. He does not want to be hampered by someone else's preferences with respect to conversation or a place to stop. He wants to be free.

Stevenson wholeheartedly agreed with William Hazlitt's essay, "On Going on a Journey." In fact, Stevenson claimed the essay was so good "that there should be a tax levied on all who have not read it."[36] However, he objected to Hazlitt's style of walking—his leaping and running with exuberance. Stevenson much preferred the steady stride that does not distract the mind and keeps the spirit open to all that is within and without. And when a fine resting spot appeared, off went the knapsack and he would sit under a tree to relax and enjoy the warm sun and surrounding birdsong. He concluded, "If you are not happy, you must have an evil conscience."[37]

Stevenson had an antipathy to clocks. He once said, "I know a village where there are hardly any clocks, where no one knows more the days of the week than by a sort of instinct for the fete on Sundays, and where only one person can tell you the day of the month, and she is generally wrong." He went on to say that if people really knew how many "armful of spare hours" such a village contained, there would certainly be a stampede to get there.[38]

Stevenson sums up "Walking Tours" by observing that so many people are so busy in their hectic lives that they run about like "frightened sheep," forgetting how simple life was meant to be lived. He would live not confined by clocks; he would be free. And when the evening was gone, he could not wait for tomorrow's travel and the new adventure before him.

Spring is not ushered in by the clock. You know when it arrives because you are walking around with the grime of winter sticking to your soul and suddenly a zephyr wafts the first whiff of lilacs straight through your nostrils and down into the nostalgic spring times of long ago and far away.

Sam Keen
Hymns for
an Unknown God

Thought to Ponder

Unlike Robert Louis Stevenson, many of us in the western world have become slaves to the clock. Our life is rigidly scheduled. What practical steps could you take to simplify and to free your own life?

Prayer

Liberating Lord, teach me to walk in such a way that I will not be constantly hampered by the dictates of the clock. Show me there is another more exciting view of time, one that is not structured but is open to the movement of your Spirit. May I walk at liberty guided by your Word in the name of Jesus, whose time was always in your hands. Amen.

MAY THERE BE A ROAD

Louis L'Amour (1908-1988)

*And I will turn all my mountains
into a road.*

ISAIAH 49:11

No one loved books more than Louis L'Amour, but his creative life was stifled by a lack of formal schooling. He had left high school in Jamestown, North Dakota, before graduation and began what he later called his "knockabout" years. He lived the life of a hobo crossing Texas on the Southern Pacific Railroad. He herded cattle. He won and lost prizefights, mostly winning. He even shipped out as a merchant seaman to far-off places, including the West Indies, England, Singapore, and China.

Everywhere L'Amour traveled, he found books to read. During those early years, he read hundreds of books, teaching himself, and preparing himself to become a writer of short stories and novels—all related to the frontier in one way or another.

What is evident in reading about L'Amour's life is the pivotal role walking played in his literary creativity. He walked all the time. Being a messenger boy was his first job, but since he did not own a bicycle he had to deliver his Western Union messages on foot. In his knockabout years, more often than not he would walk if he had a choice. Once, when his borrowed car broke down as he attempted to cross the scorching Mojave Desert in Southern California, he hiked for two days, averaging roughly three miles an hour, until he arrived at a safe destination. Arriving in Oklahoma, with the intention of becoming a writer of short stories, he revealed, "Much of my thinking during this period was done in my evening walks, usually along the road but often into a small forest of blackjack [a kind of scrub oak] nearby."[39]

A part of the thrill of the open road comes from the knowledge that leaving home can be a time of self-discovery.

Sara Covin Juengst
The Road Home

Before long, L'Amour had written more than a hundred short stories, and now he was ready to plunge into writing longer works, namely his frontier novels that eventually totaled eighty-six books, including *Hondo, The Lonesome Gods, The Walking Drum,* and the popular seventeen *Sackett* family novels. The theme of walking appears throughout his work.

In *The Warrior's Path*, one of the characters makes clear: "We who walk the woodland paths know that all men look, not many see. It is not only to keep the eyes open but to see what is there and understand."[40]

In *The Lonely Man*, someone exclaims, "Living a life is much like climbing mountains—the summits always appear further off than you think, but when a man has a goal, he always feels he's working toward something."[41]

The American land was vast, so people were lured always to find new places and try new things. There was always a horizon.

Martin Marty
Pilgrims in Their Own Land

In *The Walking Drum*, L'Amour has a character reflect his own spirit by saying, "The call of the horizon finds quick response in the heart of the wanderer."[42]

L'Amour traipsed in cities and in towns, but most of all he loved to wander in the wild country. It made no difference to him whether it was in the mountains or in the desert. He might start out exploring in his four-wheel-drive vehicle, but invariably he would get out and walk because he wanted to get a good look at artifacts, even if it meant crawling through crevasses to get what he desired.

As the title of L'Amour's memoir, *Education of a Wandering Man*, indicates, his whole life consisted of moving from one frontier to another. We capture his spirit in a watchword that sums up his philosophy in the closing paragraph of the memoir. Describing the desolate and mysterious region of Tibet and its environs he explains:

> . . . when one party meets another on the way, the greeting is often *"May there be a road!"* It is a land of frequent snow slides, rockslides, and cave-ins. Roads are casually made; bridges are usually hanging from ropes, so the saying is apropos: One hopes the way will be clear, the road open. So as one pilgrim to another, I leave you with that wish: "May there be a road."[43]

The "wandering man" impels us to persevere in our travels no matter what the adversity might be, certain that despite the obstacles before us, we ultimately will arrive at our destination.

Thought to Ponder

Louis L'Amour has sounded the note of hope for us all. We can believe that despite the roadblocks in front of us a way will open for us. Think back in your own personal experience of a time when it appeared that insurmountable obstacles stood in your way but somehow God enabled you to overcome them. Describe what happened and share your story with someone else.

Prayer

O God, guide me, especially when the way ahead does not seem to be clear. May the maxim "may there be a road" not be merely wishful thinking but grounded in my awareness of your providence in times past. I pray in the name of Jesus who is the way. Amen.

POLITICIANS
&
TEACHERS

A Comic Outline . . .
Hiking along the Roads

Abraham Lincoln (1809-1865)

But he knows the way that I take;
when he has tested me, I shall come out like gold.

Job 23:10

If you are not a coordinated walker, you probably can identify with Abraham Lincoln. Although he was a persistent walker everywhere he lived, he often made people laugh when they saw him striding from one place to the next. Biographer Carl Sandburg described him as "a comic outline against the sky he was, hiking along the roads . . . yet with a portent of a shadow."[1]

Lincoln's law partner and close friend in Springfield, Illinois, William Herndon, had this to say about Lincoln's style of walking: "When he walked he moved cautiously but firmly; his arms and giant hands swung down by his side. He walked with an even tread, the inner sides of his feet being parallel. He put the whole foot flat down on the ground at once, not rising from the toe, and hence he had no spring to his walk. . . . The whole man, body and mind, worked slowly, as if it needed oiling."[2]

Phineas Gurley, pastor of the New York Avenue Presbyterian Church in Washington, D.C., where Abraham and his wife Mary attended regularly, claimed that Lincoln walked as if "he was about to plunge forward, from his right shoulder, for he always walked, when he had anything in his hand, as if he was pushing something in front of him."[3]

Born in Hardin County, Kentucky, on February 12, 1809, Lincoln moved with his family to southern Indiana when he was seven years old. In 1818 his mother Nancy Hanks died, and his father Thomas traveled back to Kentucky to approach the widow Sarah Johnson to marry him. She agreed, and she became a beloved mother to Abraham.

In 1831, Lincoln's family moved once again, this time to the Illinois prairie. After helping to get his family

As the little girl said to the her minister, "Pastor, if you think the Lord moves in mysterious ways, you should see my mother doing aerobics." Walking is as good as an aerobic workout, as jogging or sprinting, racquetball or tennis.

Leonard Sweet
The Jesus Prescription
for a Healthy Life

73

[Edward Payson] Weston's first long-distance walk was from Boston to Washington D.C., in 10 days—the idea being to arrive in the capital in time for Lincoln's inauguration. He made Washington, but missed the ceremony by a few hours. We might add that he did attend the inauguration ball in the evening and met the president. Thus, began the remarkable career of "The Pedestrian"—the greatest long-distance walker of his day.

John Man
Walk!

settled, Abraham ventured forth on his own to the town of New Salem on the Sangamon River in search of a job. He worked as a clerk in a grocery store for a while, and later he gained employment as a surveyor in Springfield. Lincoln continued his reading and he decided to become a lawyer. On March 1, 1837, he obtained a license to practice law and he soon made a name for himself as one of Springfield's most promising lawyers.

When Mary Todd came to town from Lexington, Kentucky, Lincoln's life changed abruptly. Almost from the first time they met the two seemed attracted to each other, but their courtship was anything but smooth. Lincoln was not certain he should marry Todd. He went back and forth trying to make a decision. To resolve his dilemma, he walked the streets of Springfield attempting to figure out what he should do. Finally, he decided on marriage, and the wedding took place in Springfield on November 4, 1842.

Lincoln proceeded to practice law, and he eventually became interested in politics. He served in the House of Representatives for one term. Later, he chose to run for the U.S. Senate, but he was defeated by the popular Democratic candidate Stephen Douglas. In the 1860 presidential election, Lincoln was a dark horse candidate at the Republican convention in Chicago; however, in the end he was nominated. His winning the election in 1860 led the Southern states to secede from the Union over the issue of slavery, and the bloody Civil War ensued. Throughout the struggle, from 1861 to 1865, Lincoln persisted in his regular practice of walking about Washington, D.C., notably when he faced crucial decisions. Shocking those men who were pledged to protect him, he would frequently escape their watch and meander around the capital unarmed and seemingly afraid of no one.

Probably no other walk revealed the character of the president more than the symbolic walk he made through the streets of Richmond, Virginia, early in April 1865, shortly before the war ended. Sandburg provides the details:

Jefferson Davis had already left the city, but many people remained in the city who were still hostile toward Lincoln. Instead of riding triumphantly through the fallen Southern capitol on a horse or in a carriage, Lincoln chose to walk the two miles from the dock into the heart of the city. He had with him his son and twelve sailors. He did not wait for the army officers who were suppose to guard him as he entered this hostile city. It was a quiet, solemn procession and he walked fearlessly as an astonished crowd lined the streets.[4]

Although Lincoln's choice that day might have been considered foolish by many people, this symbolic march revealed the inner spirit of the man as perhaps nothing else could. He had no bitterness in his heart. His slow, solemn two-mile walk through Richmond showed how he really felt about the Southern folks. This was one time when Abraham Lincoln's walk did not seem funny at all.

Thought to Ponder

Lincoln "walked the talk." Where did Lincoln get the spirit of compassion and forgiveness that enabled him to walk through the hostile streets of Richmond? What resources do you need to exhibit a similar caring heart in your own time and place?

Prayer

Gracious God, grant to me a spirit of compassion and forgiveness toward those who have wronged or hurt me. Help me to forgive my enemies in the same way Jesus taught his disciples to do. Amen.

POINT-TO-POINT WALKS

Theodore Roosevelt (1858-1919)

Strengthen the weak hands,
and make firm the feeble knees.
Say to those who are of a fearful heart,
"Be strong, do not fear! Here is your God."

ISAIAH 35:3-4

What would you think of a man who, traveling in the American wilderness, had himself lowered down by a rope two hundred feet over a cliff to take a photograph from a precise position? When his companions lacked the strength to pull him up after the picture was taken, they debated for two hours until the man hanging from the rope insisted that he be dropped some forty feet into an icy stream. He was pulled out of the water half conscious, but within several days he was back resuming his pursuit of "the strenuous life."[5]

The man, so described by Edward Wagenknecht, was Theodore Roosevelt. Everything he did, he did with gusto. He had incredible energy, and he expected others to follow his example.

Reared in a prosperous home with all of its advantages, young Theodore lacked only for good health. In his early years he suffered terribly from acute asthma. Many a night his father stayed up with him into the early hours of the morning as the young boy struggled to catch his breath. He also had poor eyesight and wore glasses most of his life.

After graduating from Harvard University in 1880, Roosevelt entered politics. The people elected him to the New York Senate Assembly at the tender age of twenty-three. Later, President Benjamin Harrison appointed him civil service commissioner. In 1895 he became president of the Board of Police Commissioners in New York City. He served as assistant secretary of the Navy, led the charge up San Juan Hill in Cuba during the Spanish-American War in 1898, and returned home a war hero. Elected governor of New York, he rapidly gained national prominence as a Republican leader. President McKinley selected him as his running mate for his second term. When McKinley was assassinated, Roosevelt took the oath of office on September 14, 1901.

As president, Roosevelt defied the major corporations of his day; he broke up the trusts that stifled competition. He became an ardent champion of conservation and set aside large areas of land to be protected by the federal government and free from private economic development. He played an active role in world affairs, and even gained a Nobel Peace Prize in 1906 for his work as mediator in a dispute between Russia and Japan. After his second term he retired temporarily from politics and went on a hunting expedition in Africa. He re-entered politics as a third party candidate against Woodrow Wilson in the 1912 election, but he was badly defeated. He died of a blood clot in 1919.

Roosevelt had walked long distances since his early years. In his autobiography he recalled, "I was fond of walking and climbing. As a lad I used to go to the north woods, in Maine, both in fall and winter."[6]

During his years as president, he did not curtail his active outdoor life. He had the habit of inviting his guests to go with him on what he called his "point-to-point" walks. He did not amble along leisurely; his walks consisted of overcoming one obstacle after another.

He wrote his son Kermit a letter, dated February 16, 1908, indicating that he had taken some of his friends, including Colonel Lyon of Texas, for a walk down Rock Creek. The walk involved climbing huge rocks and Roosevelt ventured to swim in the frigid creek. Colonel Lyon balked. In this case, Roosevelt was reluctant to press his guest further, writing to his son in the letter, "I was afraid to let him when I found he was doubtful as to his ability to get over; for I did not want a guest to drown on one of my walks."[7]

Such was the daring and stamina of Theodore Roosevelt that he would walk anywhere for long distances and, if obstacles were in the way, he found a means to get around them. He believed fiercely in "the strenuous life."

Thought to Ponder

Theodore Roosevelt believed heartily in what was called in his day "muscular Christianity." He was determined to put his faith into action whether it was fighting the trusts in the field of commerce or battling on behalf of the wilderness by creating national parks. As you seek to translate your faith into action today, what do you see as the most pressing issues of the twenty-first century?

Prayer

O God, may I not be content just to enjoy private fellowship with you, comforting and fulfilling at it may be. Rather, keep me alert to see practical ways I can relate my personal faith to everyday problems. Even when my hands are weak and my knees feeble, you have promised that your strength will energize my fearful heart. Amen.

SOME OF THE GREAT TRAILS
OF OUR NATIONAL TRAILS SYSTEM

1. The Appalachian Trail
2. The Potomac Heritage Trail
3. The Daniel Boone Trail
4. The Florida Trail
5. The Lewis and Clark Trail
6. The Mormon Pioneer Trail
7. The Oregon Trail
8. The Pacific Crest Trail
9. The Continental Divide Trail

Mort Malkin
Walking—The Pleasure Exercise

As If You Are Going Some Place

Harry S. Truman (1884-1972)

Let your eyes look directly forward,
and your gaze be straight before you.
Keep straight the path of your feet,
and all your ways will be sure.

PROVERBS 4:25-26

Ralph Keyes, in his *Wit and Wisdom of Harry Truman,* describes the president's last press conference with reporters who had been with him the past seven years. He appreciated the frank discussions they had during this time, but he could not resist chiding them by saying, "Since 1945, when I came up here to the White House, I have taken a thousand and two morning walks. Some of you went on one or two, but you didn't go on any more."[8]

The crusty Harry S. Truman had spoken his mind one more time. He always confronted adverse circumstances head on. He knew that his particular work in the political sphere would not be conducive to physical fitness unless he made a determined effort to find a way to maintain good health. For him, it would be early morning daily walks.

The former senator from Missouri was selected in 1944 as Franklin D. Roosevelt's running mate when the president sought an unprecedented fourth term in office. When Roosevelt died suddenly at Warm Springs, Georgia, on April 12, 1945, Truman became president. Many people thought this relatively unknown man with a sharp tongue and a rather undignified demeanor would not be equal to the job. The well-read, honest, hardworking Truman fooled his critics. He worked together with U.S. allies and their leaders, Churchill and Stalin, to bring World War II to a successful conclusion. He also made the awesome decision to drop the atomic bomb on Hiroshima and Nagasaki; that decision ended the war with the official Japanese surrender on November 2, 1945.

Truman proved to be astute as a post-war president, developing the Truman Doctrine to combat the spread

Historically, dedicated walkers have always known the value of walking sticks—Moses and Socrates, Benjamin Franklin and Henry David Thoreau, Harry S. Truman and Winston Churchill. . . . You find yourself falling into a natural rhythm as the stick coordinates with the motion of your legs.

Mark Bricklin, editor
Walking for Health

of communism, and instituting the Marshall Plan that provided aid for the economic recovery of Europe. In 1948 he ran for reelection, and he astounded all the experts by defeating the heavily favored Republican nominee, Thomas Dewey, in one of the most extraordinary upsets in U.S. political history. During his second term, he, along with representatives from eight other nations, created the North Atlantic Treaty Organization to defend Western Europe and, in 1950, he led the United States into the Korean Conflict to confront the advance of communist North Korea into South Korea.

As early as his first days in the U.S. Senate, Truman began his daily practice of early morning walks in Washington, D.C. He walked primarily for his physical health. He unfailingly arose each morning to take his strolls—usually half an hour as he covered his customary two miles. He would swing his arms with great force and take deep breaths as he traveled 120 paces a minute. No one could fail to notice that he walked with a sense of purpose. Keyes asserted that Truman's philosophy of walking could be summed up this way: "If you are going to walk for your physical benefit, it is necessary that you walk as if you are going some place."[9]

Truman knew where he was going and he knew what it took to get there. Walking was indispensable to his physical and mental health and he was an outspoken advocate of what he called his "daily constitutionals." He would get up as early as 5:30 every morning. At first, some reporters would join him, thinking it was just a publicity stunt and they would try to keep up with the president. Most of the reporters dropped out, unable to keep pace with this vigorous older man.

Later, in his retirement when he would visit New York City, the taxi drivers who had remembered him would smile at him and shout out the door, "When are you going to ride again, Harry?" But Truman always gave his stock reply—he simply liked to walk for his health before breakfast.

Truman set a fine example of someone who took seriously the necessity of physical exercise every day, and he did it exuberantly so that everyone knew he was having a good time. This was a tradition he wanted to maintain the rest of his life.

The Abkhasians make walking a natural part of their lives. A typical day can be outlined as follows: awaken; personal hygiene; stroll; breakfast; walk to work; work; lunch; nap; work; walk home; dinner; leisure (music, visiting, etc.); evening stroll; bed.

Mort Malkin
Walking—
The Pleasure Exercise

Thought to Ponder

His contemporaries knew where Harry S. Truman was going. There was nothing strange about his style of walking. He walked as if he was "going some place." What set of disciplines have you developed in your own walk of faith that keeps you moving toward your intended goals?

Prayer

Faithful, covenant God, grant me discipline in my spiritual life even as I take for granted the need for such discipline in academic work, sports, and other facets of life. As the wisdom writer urges me, may my gaze be straight ahead bent on doing your will. Amen.

THE PATH TO ROME

Hilaire Belloc (1870-1953)

These things I remember, as I pour out my soul:
how I went with the throng,
and led them in procession to the house of God,
with glad shouts and songs of thanksgiving,
a multitude keeping festival.

PSALM 42:4

Hilaire Belloc walked throughout Europe and even across the United States from the east coast to the west coast in the 1890s, but his most memorable walk was "The Path to Rome."

Born in St. Cloud, a Paris suburb, Belloc grew up in England and, in 1903, became a British citizen. He served in Parliament from 1906 to 1910 as a member of the Liberal Party, but he soon became disillusioned with politics. He wrote widely as a poet, historian, essayist, and novelist. Before long, he joined his literary talents with G. K. Chesterton to provide a formidable defense of Roman Catholicism and conservative values in the first half of the twentieth century.

In his book *The Path to Rome,* published in 1902, Belloc describes his journey on foot from Toul in the north of France, along the Moselle River, through Switzerland, over the Alps into Italy, and to Rome, his ultimate destination. He depicts in graphic language the sights he saw and the people he met along the way, but the book is not primarily a travelogue; rather, it is a fervent account of a profound spiritual pilgrimage.

Wherever possible in his journey, Belloc searched for a church where he could start the day hearing Mass, even if it was the most humble dwelling. Once, he came upon a shrine where Mass was celebrated only on very special occasions, yet empty sacred sites like this shrine were symbolic to him because "they anchor these wild places in their own past."[10] As Belloc approached Switzerland from the Jura Mountains, he viewed the Alps—"those magnificent creatures of God"—some fifty miles away. He was captivated by their grandeur. He simply adored these great peaks that

The earliest recorded pilgrimage is accorded to Abraham, who left Ur 4,000 years ago, seeking the inscrutable presence of God in the vast desert.

Phil Cousineau
The Art of Pilgrimage

somehow linked him to his immortality. Interestingly, throughout the trip he sketched drawings of scenes he did not want to forget and included them in the book.

In the German-speaking part of Switzerland, he had difficulty communicating with the peasants as he moved through the beautiful but treacherous Bernese Oberland. Belloc mocked the tourists he encountered because their main desire seemed to be only to see the great waterfalls in the area. He was on a more serious mission and he would not be distracted by such trifles. By this time he was exhausted in his travels. His boots were worn out, with one sole flapping as he walked. Going over the Alps was more than he had bargained for, but he finally made it through St. Gotthard Pass and entered the Italian-speaking part of Switzerland. As far as Belloc was concerned he was finally in Italy.

Although he was fatigued and hungry, the weather had become warm and he was greeted by "the good people" of Italy with whom he had so much in common, in particular their shared Catholic faith. He continued on his journey until he finally arrived at the outskirts of Rome. His heart was filled with joy and anticipation. When he came to Rome itself he went to the first church he saw, Our Lady of the People. Unfortunately, Mass had just ended. He waited. In another twenty minutes mass would begin again.

The book ends as Belloc exults in poetic enthusiasm:

> Across the valleys and the high-land
> With all the world on either hand.
> Drinking when I had a mind to,
> Singing when I felt inclined to;
> Nor ever turned my face to home
> Till I slaked my heart at Rome.[11]

From the very beginning of his pilgrimage, Belloc knew where he was going. In his mind a straight line led him from where he began to where he planned to finish. Standing on a mountain top he exclaimed, "They unroll themselves all in their order till I can see Europe and Rome shining at the end." No matter how winding the roads or how steep the rock climbs, he had a plan: "to march on as directly as possible toward Rome, which was my goal."[12]

Globe-trotting destroys ethnocentricity. It helps you understand and appreciate different cultures. . . . Travel changes people.

Rick Steves
Rick Steves' Amsterdam

Belloc's biographer, A. N. Wilson, sums up very well this purpose when he writes, "We know not only where he is marching to, but what he is marching for. It is a proclamation of his delight in Europe, his addiction to the past, and his happy acquiescence in its Faith."[13]

Others might have serious religious doubts, but not Belloc on this spiritual adventure. He resolved any major doubts he had earlier in life by embracing the historic Christian faith, and *The Path to Rome* affirms to all the fervent spirit and devotion of this indefatigable pilgrim.

Thought to Ponder

No one had a greater appreciation for the rich heritage of the Christian faith than did Hilaire Belloc. He especially relished the inspiration of regular worship. What were your early experiences of worship? Were they boring or enriching? Reflect upon your memories.

Prayer

Eternal God, like the psalmist, sometimes when I am forced by illness or injury to withdraw for a time from the worshiping congregation, I miss these joyful celebrations. May I meditate upon the good memories I recall of those occasions when I led your people in praise and thanksgiving. Amen.

THE MUSIC IN MY HEAD

Alfred Kazin (1915-1998)

Praise the LORD! Praise God in the sanctuary;
praise him in his mighty firmament.

PSALM 150:1

"Walking, I always knew how I felt by the music in my head."[14] In this manner, Alfred Kazin described what walking meant to him as a boy growing up in the New York City area.

Kazin would become a leading American literary critic. He graduated from the College of New York and also did graduate work at Columbia University. He was a prolific writer of essays in the field of American literature.

I have included him with the politicians because he became an expert in politics through his research and writing. He specialized in the politics of the anti-Stalinist left. Unlike other Jewish intellectuals of the 1940s and 1950s, however, he did not look to Europe for his political standards, but rather focused on the American experience.

His first book, *On Native Grounds*, published in 1942, was a study of American prose literature from William Dean Howells to William Faulkner. He also wrote a variety of essay collections including *The Inmost Leaf* (1955), *Contemporaries* (1962), *Bright Book of Life* (1973), *An American Procession* (1984), *Writing Was Everything* (1995), and *God & the American Writer* (1997).

Kazin also wrote autobiographical works including *A Walker in the City*, published in 1951. In his later book, *Writing Was Everything*, he tells of walking the London streets shortly after World War II reciting the poetry of William Blake. He realized he was walking the same streets that the gifted poet once walked. When he returned to New York, he decided he would write about walking in his own city.

Kazin describes the profound effect walking had upon his early life, a time when he battled stuttering and the fear of public speaking in class. Growing up in Brownsville, Kazin had difficulty in school, especially when he was called upon to speak in class. Due to his stuttering, he dreaded when teachers turned to him and

> *The great advantage of walking is that it can be done anywhere by anyone, regardless of age or sex.*
>
> *Kenneth Cooper, M.D.*
> The Aerobics Program for
> Total Well-Being

Patsy Cline's first big hit, "I go out walking, after midnight," was recorded on November 8, 1956, but the record company did not release it right away. Patsy sang it first publicly on the Arthur Godfrey Talent Show to instant fame, and the record company released it soon after her radio debut.

www.patsy.nu/main.html

asked him questions. When he was outside walking, however, everything seemed to be different. Only then did he feel confident and free. "Only when I was alone in the open air, pacing the roof with pebbles in my mouth, as I had read Desmothenes had done to cure himself of stammering, or in the street, where all words seem to flow from the length of my stride."[15] It was walking that enabled him to overcome his challenges and prepare for a highly successful academic and literary career.

Kazin recalled the thrill of trudging across the Brooklyn Bridge on a dark winter day when he was fourteen years old. "The whole bridge seemed to shake under the furious blows of the crowd starting for home."[16]

One of young Alfred's favorite destinations was the new public library. After supper while it was still light he would amble through the ethnic neighborhoods until he reached the library. There he would lose himself in books, observing that not too many people had used the books he was reading or borrowing. What a delightful hideaway for him, "but even better was the long walk out of Brownsville to reach it."[17]

The "best of all walks," however, was the promenade to Highland Park. We can imagine why when he tells us he was sixteen and she was fifteen. He would meet her, and they would mosey for hours around the park. Then they would lie down on the grass and watch the lights from the great city below. He remembered:

> When we went home taking us past the cemetery, with the lights of Jamaica Avenue spread out before us, it was hard to think of them as something apart, they were searching out so many new things in me.[18]

Alfred Kazin's boyhood walks inspired him to overcome his troublesome stuttering and prepared him for an extraordinary writing career as an adult. His remedy for conquering the blues was simply stated in *A Walker in the City:*

> You had only to shake a leg, take up a book to read on the long subway ride, and get off anywhere, walk it off—not ashamed to think your own thoughts, to sing, to meet beautiful unmet Chassidim, even to pray as you pleased. Walking, I always knew how I felt by the music in my head.[19]

Thought to Ponder

Alfred Kazin was most free when he was outdoors walking, a time when he heard "music in my head." Martin Luther once wrote: "Next after theology I give to music the highest place and the greatest honor." Mull over in your mind what role music plays in your walk of faith.

Prayer

Like the psalmist, O God, I praise you not only inside in the sanctuary but also outside amid your mighty firmament. I thank you for the gift of music you have given to certain people within the believing community who lead the rest of us in lifting our hearts in hymns of praise. Surely we are meant to have a lilt to our faith. Amen.

HALFWAY DOWN THE HILL

Clare Boothe Luce (1903-1987)

Even though I walk through the darkest valley,
I fear no evil; for you are with me;
your rod and your staff—they comfort me.

PSALM 23:4

How often are we not certain whether our actions are an impulsive whim or perhaps in some way related to God's providence? At the time, it may seem to be the former, but from a later perspective, we may discern God's hand at work in our baffling experience. Something like that happened to Clare Boothe Luce when she walked "halfway down the hill" with her daughter Ann one Sunday morning. But first, we need to know something about this exceptional woman.

Luce was born in New York City. Her ambitious mother guided her into a marriage with a wealthy man when she was quite young. After Clare divorced her alcoholic husband some years later, she became rich and lived a glamorous life. She also became a successful playwright; her most triumphant play was the biting satire *The Woman,* first staged in 1936.

In 1935, Clare married Henry Luce, the powerful and influential founder of *Time, Life,* and *Fortune* magazines. She would go on to play a pioneering role for women in politics. She served as a Republican from Connecticut in the U.S. House of Representatives from 1943 to 1947. She also was appointed U.S. ambassador to Italy and still later ambassador to Brazil.

Clare showed superb athletic skills even as a young child and, as she grew older, frequently surpassed men as well as women in swimming, horsemanship, and other related sports activities. She was also a diligent walker throughout her lifetime. As a young girl she often took three-hour daily walks to trim down her weight while vacationing at the Connecticut shore.

One summer vacation, as she contemplated applying to Columbia University's School of Journalism, she had a mystical episode that she remembered into her adult years. Her biographer Sylvia Jakes Morris describes the encounter:

James Hocking of Teaneck, New Jersey, who, in 1924, at the age of 68, walked from Coney Island to San Francisco in 75 days, averaging 50 miles a day.

John Man
Walk!

One day walking along the beach, religious ecstasy enveloped her—a brief but unforgettable moment of exaltation when she knew "all there was to know of life, and death, and the Trinity," and had "the feeling that God had touched my face, and I had touched His."[20]

As an adult, Luce kept up her walking. She enjoyed ambling with her husband in such resort locales as Phoenix, Arizona, and along the beaches in Hawaii.

Stephen Shadegg, in his study of Luce's life, tells of her most transforming walk. It took place one Sunday morning, January 9, 1944, to be exact, when she and her daughter Ann left their San Francisco hotel and descended a steep hill on foot. As they passed a small Catholic church, on an impulse Ann suggested they attend the service. They stayed through the Mass and then they meandered down the hill to the St. Francis Hotel for breakfast.

The next day, while Ann was on her way back to Stanford University, she was killed in a car accident. Luce was devastated. She retraced her steps and went halfway down the hill again to the Catholic church where Ann and she had worshiped. She felt that there must be some meaning in Ann's wanting to attend that particular service when neither one of them had planned on doing so originally. Crushed in spirit, she tried to pray. The only prayer she knew was the Lord's Prayer and even that did not seem to help. She realized she did not have a solid faith to see her through this tragedy. Talking to the priest did not seem to assuage her doubts and pain either, but he did recommend that she get in touch with Fulton Sheen, the great apologist of the Catholic faith. She contacted Sheen and he gently led her through her grief into a deeper understanding of the Christian faith.[21]

As Luce looked back on that moment of serendipity, she always believed it was more than happenstance that compelled her daughter to stop that Sunday morning halfway down the hill to attend that exact service. In the midst of her doubts and despair she came to know the reality of God.

For believers, another means of making a pilgrimage has presented itself through the Internet. 'Virtual pilgrimage' is now a relatively common phenomenon.

James Harpur
Sacred Tracks

Thought to Ponder

Looking back over the past year you probably now detect that God's hand guided you in a special way that you did not realize at the time. What does the promise of Psalm 23 say to you as you contemplate the crises that might lie ahead for you?

Prayer

Living God, I trust your providence to guide me through even the darkest valley, believing that your shepherd's care will be with me until I walk in the sunshine once again. Amen.

WANDERJAHR

Arnold J. Toynbee (1889-1975)

Thus says the LORD: Stand at the crossroads, and look,
and ask for the ancient paths, where the good way lies;
and walk in it, and find rest for your souls."

JEREMIAH 6:16

Arnold J. Toynbee's magisterial twelve volume series *A Study of History* made a tremendous impact upon his contemporaries. The concept of "challenge and response" was at the heart of his comparison of twenty-six major civilizations as he traced each one's rise and fall in history. Toynbee argued that civilizations tended to disintegrate when their leaders were unable to respond to certain religious and moral challenges that came their way.

Toynbee was born in London, England, and he studied at the elite Winchester public school and then at Balliol College, Oxford University, achieving superior grades at both institutions. He came from a distinguished family that included his uncle and namesake, Arnold Toynbee, whose work as a leading social reformer and economist was sparked by a fervent Christian social conscience. Arnold J's family, however, had fallen on hard times. By the time the young man began his academic studies, he was forced to work diligently to earn scholarships to ensure his education. His father eventually was committed to a mental institution.

In Toynbee's senior year at Oxford, he won the coveted Jenkins Prize, which enabled him to travel in Italy and Greece for almost a year free of charge. Toynbee's mother, Edith, had a pronounced effect upon his life from his early years. She constantly read to him and instilled in him a love of history. Furthermore, his mother—a formidable walker all of her life—encouraged her son to pursue rigorous physical exercise. Although he hated team sports and did not do well in them, he did develop his physical strength, excelling in cross-country walking.

His biographer, William H. McNeill, comments on his passion for physical exercise: "An extraordinary appetite for seeing new places, talking with local inhabitants, and using his leg muscles to climb up hills and

> *To my Mother who understood that walking for fun is no crazier than most things in life, and who passed the information along.*
>
> Colin Fletcher
> The Complete Walker IV

Fred Miller, President of the Tuscarawas County Historical Society (eastern Ohio), a teacher at heart, puts his walking to good use. He leads evening walks through cemeteries in the county telling fascinating stories about the founding fathers and mothers of each locale.

explore the countryside stayed with him well into his old age."[22]

Toynbee's *Wanderjahr* in Italy and Greece (1911 to 1912; actually a span of nine months) heightened his earlier love of walking. The Jenkins Prize allowed him without extra expense to trek about Europe, taking in cultural and aesthetic sights not accessible through just reading books. This walking tour had an extraordinary influence on his later scholarship and teaching methods. Henceforth, he would be able to teach not solely by exhaustive academic research. He would instead illuminate his teaching with firsthand experience of the subject matter. And so he left Oxford to tramp through the country of Greece.

What a thrill it was for Toynbee to travel more than two thousand miles, walking in the footsteps of Socrates, Plato, and Aristotle. He came to know and appreciate his Greek mentors in a deeper sense than he ever could have through mere book learning. This exhilarating seasoning provided him with the inspiration for his later brilliant interpretation of the ancient Greco-Roman civilization. From the beginning, he had a clear-cut goal in finishing his Greek education. In his autobiography, *Experiences*, he wrote of the tingle of excitement he had "seeing with my own eyes, for the first time, the physical landscape of the Greek world that had become my spiritual home. . . . This year of hiking would supply the hitherto missing element in my Greek education."[23] He took his time viewing the sites of the ancient city-states, noting carefully just how long it took his heroes to travel on foot from place to place in this rugged country.

Toynbee was convinced he was doing the right thing in pursuing the walking tour. He summed up his dazzling year in these words:

> One's own feet were the right means of conveyance for this purpose. In walking, I was following in the footsteps of the ancient Greeks themselves; for they too, had walked—even the most eminent of them—so I was traveling in the way in which they had traveled, and was moving at their pace.[24]

The importance of this *Wanderjahr* in Toynbee's life cannot be overestimated. Suffice to say, he was a different man after that grand tour. His prodigious book learning was now joined with personal experience that would forever change his outlook on life and history. The *Wanderjahr* transformed him, providing the stimulus for his later work as the preeminent philosopher of history.

Thought to Ponder

When young Arnold J. Toynbee left the classroom for his grand tour of Greece, his academic work came alive and his walk made an indelible mark upon him. As a student what areas of life do you need to explore to find similar stimulation to realize your own goals?

Prayer

O God our help in ages past, our help for years to come, help me to plumb the rich tradition of my particular family of faith. Like the ancient prophet declares, may I search for the ancient paths to shed light on my journey today. Amen.

Walking Alone to Signal Hill

Frank Laubach (1884-1970)

For we walk by faith, not by sight.

2 Corinthians 5:7

Frank Laubach came to be known as the "Teacher of Millions" through his original literacy teaching methods, which have taught countless numbers of people in developing countries to read. In 1929, however, his world seemed to be at a standstill. He was a defeated man, a burnt-out missionary serving in the Philippines, certain that he would never accomplish what he set out to do, namely make a difference in the lives of the people he had come to help.

Laubach had a promising start. He grew up in the tiny town of Benton, in north central Pennsylvania, in a devout and supportive family. He went to Princeton University and then to Union Theological Seminary in New York, eventually gaining a Ph.D. in sociology at Columbia University. His dissertation focused on research he had done among a hundred vagrant men connected to the City Mission Society in New York City.

In 1914, as an ordained minister of the Congregational Church, he and his wife Effa left the United States. They sailed to the Philippines where he labored at Mindanao. Frank and Effa saw their first three children die of malaria and dysentery. Robert, their only surviving child, was taken away by Effa to the United States for a period of time to regain his physical strength during an outbreak of severe illness. Effa and Robert eventually came back and assisted Laubach in his mission work.

Even though Laubach spent much time writing, teaching, and serving where he could, he did not feel he was doing much good. He suffered keen disappointment when he lost a close election to become the president of Union Theological Seminary in Manila.

On December 1, 1929, Laubach arrived in Lanao, a place he had originally gone to fifteen years before. On his first visit he was asked to leave because of the distrust of the U.S. armed forces in the area. Even now, as he returned, he sensed a strong resistance among the

> *I had better admit right away that walking can in the end become an addiction, and that it is then as deadly in its fashion as heroin or television or the stock exchange. But even in this final stage it remains a delectable madness, very good for sanity, and I recommend it with a passion.*
>
> *Colin Fletcher*
> The Complete Walker III

Maranao people to his Christian message. The largely Muslim population did not take kindly to any effort at conversion.

One evening he took a walk alone to Signal Hill. From his vantage point on the hill high above the village, he observed the homes of the Maranao people below. He wondered how he could reach these people. All that he had heard about them convinced him they were dirty, illiterate, some of them even murderous. Each evening he would climb Signal Hill to be alone to pray for guidance and each day he came to the same conclusion that he would never be able to help these people.

Finally, after many days of ascending Signal Hill, his answer came. God seemed to be saying to him:

Many, I think, are prayer-walking because it's easy and natural and very, very basic—once you get the hang of it: you put one foot in front of the other; you take one conscious breath after another; you speak to God and let God speak to you, or embrace you, one word, one embrace, after another . . . and another.

Linus Mundy
The Complete Guide to
Prayer-Walking

> My child you have failed because you do not really love these Moros. You feel superior to them because you are white. If you can forget you are an American and think only how I love them, they will respond. . . . If you want the Moros to be fair to your religion, be fair to theirs. Study the Koran with them.[25]

Laubach came down the hill and told the leaders of the Moros that he wanted to study the Koran. Dialogue ensued. Barriers broke down and Laubach had the opportunity to learn their language. As he listened to their oral traditions, he realized no one had written down the language, which he proceeded to do. When the Moros saw what he had done, they begged him to teach them how to read their own language.

That was the origin of Laubach's unique literacy teaching methods, which in time enabled people all over the world to learn to read. In April 1949, *Life* magazine credited him with teaching sixty million people to read.[26] He traveled extensively, well into his eighties, challenging Americans not to forget "the silent billion" illiterate people in the world who lived for the most part in poverty and disillusionment.

During those early years of mission and literacy work in the Philippines, Laubach returned repeatedly to that place that symbolized the turning point in his life—Signal Hill. In his *Letters by a Modern Mystic,* Laubach wrote on May 24, 1930, "The day has been rich but strenuous, so I climbed 'Signal Hill' back of my house talking and listening to God all the way up, all the way back, all the lonely half hour on the top. And God talked back."[27]

On June 22, 1930, he mentioned in another letter:

I have just returned from a walk alone, a walk so wonderful that I feel like reducing it to a universal rule that all people ought to walk every evening all alone where they can talk aloud without being heard by anyone, and during this entire walk they all ought to talk with God, allowing Him to use their tongues to talk back—and letting God do most of the talking.[28]

Laubach also encouraged fellow Christians to learn to "flash" intercessory prayers to people near and far believing that not a few of these prayers will hit their mark.

During the rest of his life, Laubach followed the practice of being aware of the presence of God in all kinds of circumstances. Walking, in particular, seemed to be the activity where he most frequently established such contact. Nothing compared to those early experiences of hiking to the top of Signal Hill when Frank Laubach's life was forever altered.

Thought to Ponder

Frank Laubach also claimed that what young people needed more than long prayers or long sermons was to learn how to make brief sentence prayers and then send these "flash prayers" to others and watch such intercessions change lives. Who are the people who need your intercessory prayers? Your family? Your friends? Your teacher? Your coach? Your pastor? National or world leaders?

Prayer

Sovereign God, may I be aware of your presence with me on my daily walk. Others may not see what is happening, but I "walk by faith, not by sight." Assist me in sending "flash prayers" of your love toward everyone I meet today. Amen.

THE THREE FRIENDS WALKED
ROUND AND ROUND

C. S. Lewis (1898-1963)

Teach me your way, O LORD
that I may walk in your truth.

PSALM 86:11

When C. S. Lewis died the newspapers and the television media did not give him the coverage he might ordinarily have had because that same day, November 22, 1963, John F. Kennedy, president of the United States, was assassinated in Dallas, Texas. Also, the noted English author Aldous Huxley died in Los Angeles the same day.

Nonetheless, nothing can be taken away from the distinguished life of Lewis, a brilliant Oxford professor, known not only in academic circles for his extraordinary poetry and prose, but also appreciated for his *The Chronicles of Narnia,* a magical fantasy that has enthralled generations of children long after the author's death.

After many years as an agnostic, Lewis converted to the Christian faith and became arguably the paramount evangelical Christian apologist of the twentieth century. His many books include *The Case for Christianity, The Screwtape Letters, The Problem of Pain,* and his autobiography, *Surprised by Joy.* All are widely read throughout the English-speaking world.

Lewis was far from being an academic recluse. He was a keen walker who enjoyed the sounds and sights of the natural world. According to Clyde S. Kilby, an "ideal day" for Lewis would consist of the following schedule:

8:00 a.m.—Breakfast
9:00 a.m.–1:00 p.m.—Study and writing with perhaps a cup of tea at
  11:00.
1:00 p.m.—Lunch and after lunch a walk "preferably alone." He even left
  his precious pipe behind "in order not to miss the full odor of nature."
5:00 p.m.–7:00 p.m.—More work and then the Evening Meal, and then
  talk and light reading.
11:00 p.m.—Bedtime[29]

Even though such a schedule constituted "an ideal day" for Lewis, he needed more walking than his daily afternoon strolls. He also yearned for holidays and vacations when he could hike in the woods for hours and days. His letters are saturated with his delight in walking. To Arthur Greeves, he wrote in October 1915: "I would remember the glorious walk of which you speak, how we lay long drenched with sunshine on the moss, and were for a short time perfectly happy—which is a rare enough condition God knows."[30]

In April 1927, he embarked on an extensive tramp through the English countryside. He met three friends some twenty miles southwest of Oxford and spent the next five days exploring the area on foot. He wrote to his brother of, "the delight of coming to a sudden drop and looking down into a rich wooded valley where you see the roofs of the place where you're going to have supper and bed; especially if the sunset lies on the ridge beyond the valley."[31]

Later in his life, Lewis described a two-week "honeymoon" walk through Ireland with his wife Joy, who had only a short time to live. Despite the bittersweet two weeks, they returned to Oxford "drunk with blue mountains, yellow beaches, dark fuchsia, breaking waves, braying donkeys, peat-smell, and the heather just beginning to bloom."[32]

Of all the countless walks Lewis enjoyed during his lifetime, nothing was as eventful as the evening he and two of his friends walked round and round Addison's Walk, a circle of a mile in length at Oxford. J. R. R. Tolkien, who later would write the hugely popular *Lord of the Rings,* was one of the friends. The other was Hugo Dyson, another Oxford scholar. Tolkien embraced the Roman Catholic faith; Dyson adhered to a High Anglican Church conviction. Lewis, a confirmed agnostic at the time, had many doubts about Christianity. Lewis's two friends sought to convince him of the truth of the Christian faith. At the time, he could not see how the ancient story of Jesus could have relevance for him today. Tolkien encouraged him to use his imagination, just as he did in interpreting the ancient myths that fascinated him, except that he should believe that the story of Jesus "really happened." Lewis did not depart from his friends that night until 4:00 A.M.

Nine days later, Lewis was on a bus on the way to an outing at the zoo. It seemed like a perfectly

Two kinds of walking: Well-known Bible teacher F. Dale Bruner walks an hour each way from his home to Fuller Theological Seminary in Pasadena, California, to do scholarly research. Most afternoons he walks with his wife Kathy in the park *"so that I can learn to 'chat,' my single major challenge in life."*

F. Dale Bruner
www.fpch.org/dalebruner.htm

normal day, but as he related in his autobiographical book, *Surprised by Joy,* "When we set out I did not believe that Jesus Christ was the Son of God, and when we reached the zoo I did."[33] Still later, when he told the happy news to his friend Arthur Greeves, he referred to his previous walk in the evening and confessed, "My long night talk with Dyson and Tolkien had a good deal to do with it."[34]

One Oxford University law penalized students for night walking twice as severely as for shooting an arrow at a teacher.

Joseph A. Amato
On Foot

Thought to Ponder

God seems to send a friend at just the right moment when we need someone. How has God brought someone close to you in the time of need, even as God did for C. S. Lewis?

Prayer

Merciful God, teach me to walk in your truth. Give me an eye to discern what is true and also the will to commit myself to doing the truth. Amen.

SILENT INWARD BOMBS
BURSTING QUIETLY

Brenda Ueland (1891-1985)

For you shall go out in joy,
and be led back in peace.

ISAIAH 55:12

The enthusiastic teacher speaking to them sounded like an unusual person, and she was. She had set an international swimming record for over eighty-year-olds. She tried running up a mountain while in her eighties. She customarily walked nine miles a day. The students in her class probably did not know all these facts, but there was no doubt in their minds as they listened to her that she was consumed by her passion—teaching creative writing.

Brenda Ueland grew up in Minnesota. Her father was a lawyer and a judge; her mother was a suffrage activist in Minneapolis. Later, Brenda moved to New York City, where she became part of a bohemian community in Greenwich Village. After many years in the metropolitan area she moved back to Minnesota where she wrote two books and numerous articles and short stories She is chiefly known, however, as a long-time teacher of the art of writing. Poet and historian Carl Sandburg called her book *If You Want to Write,* "the best book ever written about how to write."[35]

As a teacher, Ueland sought to motivate her students to write with passion. She desperately wanted her students to believe in themselves, to have faith that each one had something important to say. The key was imagination. If they could only tap their imagination, they would be on their way. She realized that each one was different. Some people's imagination soared when they sewed, or refinished furniture, or washed dishes. But Ueland always shared with her students what worked best for her. Walking was the key to releasing the imagination in her life and she believed that it might just be helpful to those she was teaching.

In January 2002, Minneapolis's new mayor, R. T. Rybak, used his inaugural address to summon citizens to walk the city they love.

Joseph A. Amato
On Foot

In *If You Want to Write* she stated:

I will tell you what I have learned myself. For me a long five or six mile walk helps. And one must go alone and every day. I have done this for many years. It is at these times I seem to get re-charged. If I do not walk one day, I seem to have on the next what Van Gogh called 'the meagerness' . . . after a day or two of not walking, when I try to write I feel a little dull and irresolute.[36]

Ueland did not understand her walking habits as mere grim exercises. On the contrary, she ambled along each day with keen awareness and ardent expectation. Everything came to mind as she strolled, and she commented, "My explanation of it is that when I walk in a carefree way, without straining to get to my destination, then I am living in the present. And it is only then the creative power flourishes."[37]

Ueland did not hurry or rush just to complete a certain number of miles. She focused not on the end of the trip, whether it be eating dinner or a time of leisure to read, but rather she sought to live in the present so that her power to imagine would be unleashed. As she walked she would often learn a poem or a Shakespeare sonnet. She would say a line over and over again, and as she did she found herself relaxing in body, mind, and spirit. During these moments of contemplation she found herself walking slower and slower. It was not in expending a lot of effort that insights came, but rather the opposite—in letting the imagination take over, the insights came in abundance.

Ueland explained exuberantly what often happened as she pressed on in her slow, long-distance trek: "I never took a long, solitary walk without some of these silent, inward bombs bursting quietly: I see! I understand now! And a feeling of happiness."[38]

In her autobiography, *Me, A Memoir*, Ueland underscored what the hours of daily walking meant to her. She attributed her optimistic and cheerful outlook on life to regular hiking outdoors. She concluded, "Fine, bright pure ideas come to me from some place, from the sky, I think perhaps from God."[39]

At 74 [Edward Payson Weston] walked 1,500 miles from New York to Minneapolis in 60 days.

Gary D. Yanker
The Complete Book of
Exercise Walking

For Brenda Ueland, teacher of creative writing, the secret to opening up the imagination was going out on foot on the open road to engage in slow, long-distance walking, as she anticipated those "silent, inward bombs bursting quietly."

Thought to Ponder

Brenda Ueland knew something of what the psalmist was saying (*For you shall go out in joy, and be led back in peace.*) when she began her long, slow walks with joy and anticipation, and then returned from the walks with a deep sense of peace and satisfaction. Describe a similar walk you might have taken where you too came away with a sensation of "silent, inward bombs bursting quietly."

Prayer

O Lord, my God, when I walk with you even for a short time I realize that I will not return the same person I was as when I began my venture. You are indeed the God of surprises. I await a new adventure around the next bend. Amen.

Pilgrims
&
Seekers

WALKING IN THE FIELDS

John Bunyan (1628-1688)

*Your word is a lamp to my feet
and a light to my path.*

PSALM 119:105

John Bunyan was a dreamer who described in symbolic terms one of the most fascinating spiritual journeys from doubt to faith ever recorded.

Bunyan, a tinker's son, lived in Bedford, England, during the seventeenth century, a time of intense Puritanism. As a teenager he served in the Parliamentary Army fighting against King Charles I. By 1646, he was home, and it was there that he went through a period of inner anguish about the salvation of his soul. He vividly described his dramatic conversion in his autobiography, *Grace Abounding to the Chief of Sinners.*

Bunyan became a member of the Baptist church in Bedford; subsequently, he had a call to preach the gospel. His happy marriage ended with the death of his wife. In 1660, he was sent to jail for twelve years for preaching without a proper license. Although deeply concerned for his four young children, he would not leave his jail cell, even when he was promised his freedom if he would not preach again.

John was released in 1672, but he resumed his preaching, and he was arrested again. During his second stay in the Bedford jail he wrote his most famous work, *The Pilgrim's Progress.* This best-selling allegory of the Christian journey, with its unmistakable walking motif, became the most popular book in the English language, next to the Bible, for more than two hundred years.

The book opens with the words: "As I walked through the wilderness of this world, I lighted on a certain place where was a den, and laid me down in that place to sleep, and as I slept, I dreamed a dream."[1] In his dream, Bunyan saw a troubled man (Christian) "walking in the fields" reading a book that seemed to give him much distress.

He kept calling out to himself, "What shall I do?" Fortunately, this man meets Evangelist, who points him to the wicket gate and counsels him to flee the City of Destruction and trek toward the Heavenly City.

Along the way, Christian encounters a number of colorful characters, some of them friendly, but many of them ready to dissuade him from

How might we emulate the spirit of John Bunyan? *You might take a notebook, or just remember in your heart what your spirit is told . . . out there. Create your own book of psalms, nature poems, insights, intuitions, and prayers.*

Philip Ferranti
Hiking

continuing his pilgrimage. Obstinate and Pliable become roadblocks. Pliable even leads Christian into the horrible Slough of Despond. Help comes along the way and pulls him out. Mr. Worldly Wiseman meets him and directs him to try the way of Morality. But Evangelist arrives in time to warn him that the path of Morality cannot really meet his basic need, overcome his doubt, or lift his burden of sin.

Later Christian meets Interpreter who explains to him the true way to reach his destination and find full assurance in Christ. In a striking manner, Bunyan describes Christian's release from his burden. In his dream, he depicts Christian running up the hill with the heavy burden on his back until he comes face to face with a cross, "and as Christian came up with the cross, the burden loosed from off his shoulders, and fell from off his back, and began to tumble, and so continued to do till it came to the mouth of the sepulcher, where it fell in, and I saw it no more."[2]

Bunyan then shows that Christian, despite the relief of his burden of sin and guilt, must still face tests and dangers as he walks on his way from the City of Destruction to the Heavenly City. He must travel through the Valley of Humiliation, face the temptations of Vanity Fair, and tackle numerous obstacles and sidetracks along the way. Later, he is joined by two guides, Faithful and Hopeful; the latter tramps with Christian through the deep waters of the River of Death and enables him to pass over to the other side.

What a dream! Using the imagery of the spiritual walk Bunyan paints an unforgettable picture of the Christian pilgrim and the ongoing challenge of doubt in the life of faith.

Thought to Ponder

John Bunyan's picture of the Christian life is not a stroll down primrose lane. Rather, it is a constant struggle against doubts, temptations, and evil attacks that can only be overcome in the light of God's Word. What have been some of the doubts and conflicts in your own pilgrimage? How did you overcome them?

Prayer

Gracious God, you have called me to be a pilgrim, a wayfarer, a sojourner on the way to the eternal city. When I stumble and fall, raise me up by your powerful hand, and shed your light on my path day by day until I reach my final destination. Amen.

Pilgrim, n. A traveler who is taken seriously.

Ambrose Bierce
The Devil's Dictionary

Thawing the Ice
with His Bare Feet

John Chapman, "Johnny Appleseed" (1774-1845)

I will go before you and level the mountains.

Isaiah 45:2

John Chapman, better known as "Johnny Appleseed," has to be separated from the numerous legends that have obscured his life. The actual facts of his life are exciting enough—although we do not have any documented evidence of the details of his life from his birth in Leominster, in the Massachusetts Bay Colony, until he arrived in the Pittsburgh area of Pennsylvania, about 1797.

Chapman began planting apple trees near the town of Warren. His aim was to have apple trees bearing fruit by the time the pioneers began moving westward. Next he moved to Franklin, Pennsylvania, and planted seeds in the rich soil along French Creek. The twenty-six-year-old Chapman first appeared as a resident of Franklin in the 1800 Federal Census.

By 1804, Chapman made plans to settle in the Ohio Country. His father and his father's wife, along with their young children and his half-brother, Nathaniel, had already moved to the Marietta area and would settle in a place called Dexter City, just north of Marietta on the Ohio River. Known by many people by this time as "Johnny Appleseed," Chapman soon made a name for himself. He rarely wore shoes, even in the coldest weather. Although it was claimed that he used a tin pot for a hat, there is no credible evidence of this.

Johnny was a walker like none other. Endlessly tramping through the forests and fields sowing his apple seeds, he looked forward to a harvest at a later date. He first went to Licking Creek, east of present-day Columbus. Then he moved into Ashland and Richland counties in the central part of the Ohio Country. Although Johnny might have seemed odd to many traditional people, this man with his friendly and outgoing personality was readily welcomed into the homes of the frontier settlers.

In 1974 American David Kuntz completed walking around the world (14,500 miles) in about four years.

Gary D. Yanker
The Complete Book of Exercise Walking

He bought town lots in Mount Vernon for new apple orchards. Johnny was both a truly benevolent person who really cared for people and their needs and a shrewd businessman. Furthermore, he had good relations with the Native Americans living in the region.

What is sometimes forgotten is that Johnny had a dual purpose in his walk across the Ohio Country. He wanted to spread apple seeds to provide for the physical needs of the frontier people, but he also desired to spread the Word of God to meet the spiritual needs of the same people. In the *Johnny Appleseed Sourcebook*, Robert C. Harris describes Johnny as an extraordinary missionary "who goes barefoot, can sleep anywhere, in house or out of house, and lives upon the coarsest and most scant fare. He has actually thawed the ice with his bare feet."[3] Harris goes on to say that Johnny lent books of the "New Church" to anyone who was willing to read them.

The skin on your soles is up to ten times thicker than elsewhere on your body, for protection and padding. Unfortunately, the rest of your feet are covered with ordinary, easily damaged skin, which is why skin-related problems are the main reason people visit podiatrists.

Mark Bricklin, editor
Walking for Health

The "New Church" was founded by Emanuel Swedenborg of Sweden. His doctrine stressed loving God, serving humankind, and keeping an open mind toward other religious traditions. Johnny Appleseed resolved his own personal spiritual doubts by turning to the Swedenborgian faith. With the Bible and other pertinent literature in hand, he zealously propagated the good news to all who would listen to him.

Frequently, Johnny would stay at a lonely settler's cabin for the night and before long he would pull out his Bible and offer to read some "news right fresh from Heaven."[4] Even though many of the frontier people had a difficult time understanding the subtlety and detailed exposition of this new teaching, there was no doubt that Johnny comprehended these doctrines and firmly believed in them. Eventually, Johnny moved to Fort Wayne, Indiana, where he bought forty-two acres for another apple orchard. He died there at the age of seventy on March 18, 1845.

Even today, Johnny Appleseed continues to be remembered and honored throughout the Midwest with numerous festivals commemorating his life and legend. Historian Robert Price, who has done a superb job of separating the man from the myth, leaves us with this thought: "He had walked more miles than any other recorded borderer of his generation—now he belonged to the American trails and rivers forever."[5]

Thought to Ponder

Johnny Appleseed, fondly remembered by children and young people in many generations, had a unique ministry scattering apple seeds and the Word of God at the same time. How do you see your responsibility and your church's responsibility today in meeting the physical and spiritual needs of people at home and in distant lands?

Prayer

God of the future, I am grateful that you always go before me leveling "the mountains" if they stand in the way of accomplishing your will. Help me not to be so wrapped up in myself that I lose sight of your vision of caring for the multitudes of people in dire circumstances, both physical and spiritual. Amen.

The Way of a Pilgrim

Russian Pilgrim (Nineteenth Century)

I treasure your word in my heart,
so that I may not sin against you.

Psalm 119:11

A humble Russian man goes to worship one Sunday. He is unhappy. His life has been hard with many reversals and setbacks. He had been orphaned at an early age. His brother stole his inheritance. Though he married, within a few years his wife died.

The sermon text for the day is 1 Thessalonians 5:17, "Pray without ceasing." He is both fascinated and puzzled by these words. How is it humanly possible to pray at all times? He vows to go on a journey, walking across the wide expanse of Russia, to inquire about this matter.

We do not know much about this anonymous Russian pilgrim. His story is told in a book, *The Way of a Pilgrim,* first published in Russia in 1844. In the opening paragraph, the pilgrim describes himself: "By the grace of God I am a Christian man, by my actions a great sinner, and by calling a homeless wanderer of the humblest birth who roams from place to place. My worldly goods are a knapsack with some dried bread in it on my back, and in my breast pocket a Bible. And that is all."[6]

At first, the Russian pilgrim cannot find anyone to give him a satisfactory answer as to how one can pray without ceasing. Then one day he meets a *starets*, an elder or holy man, who teaches him the Jesus Prayer, "Lord Jesus Christ, Son of God, have mercy on me a sinner."[7] The pilgrim begins to pray this simple prayer, repeating it over and over again until it becomes a part of him. Ultimately, he can repeat it without even thinking about the words. He can say the prayer a thousand times a day.

In his own words, he tells what the prayer means to him:

Sometimes my heart would feel as though it were bubbling with joy, such lightness, freedom, and consolation were in it. Sometimes I felt a burning love for Jesus Christ and for all God's creatures. . . . Sometimes that sense of warm gladness in my heart spread throughout my whole being and I was deeply moved as the fact of the presence of God everywhere was brought home to me.[8]

The number of pilgrims coming to the catacombs increased during the fourth century, when luminaria were first constructed to add light and improve air supply, and stairways widened to help access.

James Harpur
Sacred Tracks

The pilgrim soon discovered that the Jesus Prayer was not just for celibate monks in the monastery where the prayer originated, but for people of every conceivable background. Rather than isolate him from people, this prayer gave him compassion for all the people he met on his long journey. As he traveled the countryside he eagerly taught others the marvelous secret of constant prayer.

The rest of the book consists of the Russian pilgrim's encounters with a wide variety of people who are helped by practicing the presence of God. He assists the narrow minded to overcome prejudices. He convinces a deserter of the army that he can begin again. In the last part of the book, the pilgrim enters into a dialogue with a professor in which they probe the meaning of prayer and Christian piety.

The pilgrim found an answer to the question that had disturbed him since he first began his quest on that day when he heard the apostle Paul's command, "Pray without ceasing." As he walked steadfastly across Russia, he repeated the Jesus Prayer until it became assimilated into his very being.

Repeating this prayer not only gave him inner peace, but also motivated him to reach out to everyone with the love of Christ. And, as he did, wonders appeared time and time again.

The Russian pilgrim's resolve to travel across his native land until he found an answer to the question, "How is it possible to pray without ceasing?" not only transformed his own life, but also left a legacy of the Jesus Prayer that continues to exert a positive influence on spiritual seekers today.

The best-known badge was the scallop shell, at first associated with Santiago de Compostela but later so popular it came to signify pilgrimage in general.

James Harpur
Sacred Tracks

Thought to Ponder

The anonymous Russian pilgrim memorized the Jesus Prayer as he walked across the vast expanse of Russia and had his life transformed. What particular biblical verses have you memorized and what impact have they had upon your own inner life and outreach?

Prayer

O God, grant me the earnest desire not only to read and study the Bible but also to memorize key verses and treasure them in my heart. I believe that if I do so, my life will be in tune with yours, and I will not stray from your appointed pathway. Amen.

STREET PHILOSOPHER

Søren Kierkegaard (1813-1855)

*As he was walking along, he saw Levi
son of Alphaeus sitting at the tax booth,
and he said to him, "Follow me," And
he got up and followed him.*

MARK 2:14

No matter what, do not lose the joy of walking. I walk my way to health and away from every illness every day. I have walked my way to my best ideas, and I know of no thought so burdensome that one cannot walk away from it. . . . If a person just continues to walk like this, things surely will go well."[9]

Here we have a succinct statement of Søren Kierkegaard's philosophy of walking. Unfortunately, he often was absent minded. These particular words were written in a letter to his sister-in-law, Henriette, who was crippled and would have had a hard time putting his counsel into action.

Kierkegaard, a melancholy eccentric and brilliant man, mystified most people who met him. Born in 1813, he spent almost his entire life in Copenhagen, Denmark. He grew up in a wealthy family and was greatly influenced by his domineering father. Kierkegaard studied philosophy, literature, and theology at the University of Copenhagen. In 1841, he received a *Magistri Artium,* equivalent to a modern-day academic doctorate. His family inheritance enabled him to devote himself entirely to writing.

In 1840, the year before he completed his higher education, he proposed marriage to Regine Olsen, but the following year he broke off the engagement. Although the real reason is not known, in his *Journals,* Kierkegaard seems to imply that his melancholy spirit would not make him a desirable husband. Nonetheless, he did pine for Regine for many years, even after she was married.

Kierkegaard was a prolific author. Often dubbed a Christian existentialist, he sought to show that seekers cannot know God or truth by reasoned evidence but must take what he called "a leap of faith."

His major book, *Either/Or,* written in 1843, was a monster of a book, all 838 printed pages of it. In this book, he challenged the prominent German

philosopher Hegel's rational approach to truth and began to develop some of his key existential ideas. In his book *Fear and Trembling*, also published in 1843, he focused on God's strange command to Abraham to sacrifice his son Isaac as an example of the absurdity of faith. Abraham obeyed God's command even though he did not understand it.

In his later years, Kierkegaard wrote piercing critiques of the Danish state church. His works included *Practice in Christianity, For Self-Examination,* and *Judge for Yourselves!* He argued that many Danish Christians only gave lip-service to Christ and did not take their discipleship seriously. In Kierkegaard's judgment, they lacked passion and a deep personal commitment.

Kierkegaard died in 1855. At his funeral, his nephew, Henrik Lund, interrupted the service, claiming that Kierkegaard had denounced the state church and would not have wanted his funeral in such a setting.

There is no question that walking was integral to Kierkegaard's well-being, as he indicated in the letter to his sister-in-law. He always loved to walk, even as a young child. As an adult, he strode through the streets of Copenhagen and would simply disappear into the crowds. He was known far and wide as the "street philosopher."[10] There is no doubt that walking had a positive effect upon his writing career. His walking gait set him apart from other casual strollers. He tended to be restless and lopsided, as he "hopped" along.[11] He often had a bamboo walking stick and later he carried various colorful umbrellas. His wild gestures with his arms and walking stick or umbrella invariably frightened many of his walking companions.

He walked with numerous prominent people of his day, but he also was just as likely to strike up a conversation with a stranger who happened to be going his way. He recalled that Socrates, the ancient Greek philosopher, had done the same thing in the city of Athens.

Joakim Garff, his recent biographer, labels the section on his walking habits with the title "People Bath."[12] To endure his intense intellectual activity he needed his daily "people bath," as he termed it. More often than not, he would leave his startled walking partner in a flash when an insight came to him, hurrying home to write before the insight flew away.

Walking was so popular in nineteenth century Copenhagen that the city officials had to make laws determining who had the right-of-way. (According to the police ordinance of 1810, the pedestrian who had the gutter on his right-hand side had the right-of-way.)

Joakim Garff
Søren Kierkegaard: A
Biography

Thought to Ponder

Kierkegaard required his "people bath" and it did not matter to him if the one he talked to was a close friend or a total stranger. Conversation made him come alive. What are some of the ways you could sharpen your conversation skills as you mingle with friends and strangers every day?

Prayer

God of grace and mercy, keep me seeking so when your call comes I will hear and respond even as Levi did when Jesus spoke to him. Help me to be more outgoing and sensitive to the hurts of others so that I might not pass them by, not hearing your call in their cries. I pray in the name of Jesus who taught us how to care. Amen.

Gaitologists—those who study walking styles.

Gary D. Yanker
The Complete Book of Exercise Walking

THE APOSTLE
WITH THE BLEEDING FEET

Sadhu Sundar Singh (1889-1929)

*Now as he was going along and approaching
Damascus, suddenly a light from heaven
flashed around him.*

ACTS 9:3

Sundar Singh, son of a wealthy father and a devout Hindu mother, is sent
to an American Presbyterian mission school in their north Indian village
of Rampur to be educated. He reacts violently to reading the Bible that is a
part of his daily lessons. In fact, one day, in the presence of his father, he rips
apart the gospel and burns it. Despite this dramatic act, Sundar's heart is restless, so much so, that he vows to get up the next morning at 3:00 a.m. and
pray that if there is a God he will be shown the way of salvation. If not, he
resolves to go to the railroad tracks and end his life.

Later, in his book *With and Without Christ,* he describes what happened
about 4:30 a.m. that morning as he prayed and waited. He expected to see the
incarnation of one of the Hindu deities, but instead he saw a bright light and
then, "I opened the door to see where it came from, but all was dark outside.
I returned inside, and the light increased in intensity and took the form of
a globe of light above the ground, and in this light appeared, not the form I
expected, but the living Christ whom I had counted as dead."[13] He goes on to
describe his vision in words reminiscent of the apostle Paul and his encounter
with the living Christ on the Damascus road. In the end, the old Sundar died
and a new Sundar was born with an ardent desire to serve a loving God who
had changed his life.

When fifteen-year-old Sundar shared his elation with his father, he was
rebuked and cast out of the family. A year later, Sundar was baptized and
soon sensed a call to be a *sadhu* who travels the roads.
He dressed in the traditional yellow robe and turban,
just like other Hindu *sadhus* or "holy men," but the difference was his message, the proclamation of the good
news about Jesus. He determined:

*If you want to talk the talk
you've got to walk the walk.*

Robert Gilbert
The Quotable Walker

Not to receive any money for this work; to eat when food was offered to him; to go hungry if no one gave him food; to sleep under a roof if he was invited to do so, otherwise to sleep under a tree or in a cave, or in a broken-down or vacant house. His Master had suffered for him and so he would also suffer. That would be his greatest joy—to serve and suffer for Jesus who loved him so deeply.[14]

Sundar traveled north to the Punjab and then into Kashmir, and finally into Afghanistan. He met with abuse and ridicule along the way. He suffered terribly from the weather. His bare feet were cut and bruised. He came to be known as "The Apostle with the Bleeding Feet."[15] Nevertheless, he persisted in walking along the road. When he was nineteen years old, he came to the strange and enchanted land of Tibet, noted for its isolation and strict Buddhism. He was repelled by the poverty and the uncleanness of most people. Once again, he was confronted with hostility.

The next year he roamed around India and his friends encouraged him to begin theological studies at an Anglican college in Lahore. The students at the college thought him to be odd. The academic work did not appeal to him. He found his studies, for the most part, impractical. More than ever he realized that God had not called him to a settled ministry patterned after Western customs; he felt called to be a solitary pilgrim on the road

Sometime later, Sundar returned to Tibet, but once again his witness was not appreciated. In 1918, he traveled to South India. The following year, he went to Burma, Malaysia, China, and Japan. He became widely known as a Christian mystic, a man of prayer with genuine humility. Stories circulated about his miraculous deeds and extraordinary visions. Even his most devoted friends had difficulty on occasion separating fact from fiction.

In the meantime, his aging father, who had become a Christian, provided money for his son to travel to Great Britain, the United States, and Australia. Like many spiritual leaders from the East, he was appalled by the secularism and materialism in the West.

Rather than settle down once he returned to India, he took to the open road again. It soon became apparent, however, that his health was not good. For a while

> *He was not a member of any denomination, and did not try to begin one of his own, though he shared fellowship with Christians of all kinds. He lived (to use a later phrase) to introduce his own people to "the Christ of the Indian road."*
>
> John Woodbridge on
> Sadhu Sundar Singh
> More Than Conquerors

he slowed down and spent time praying and writing, but then in 1929, despite his ill health and warnings from his friends, he unwisely set out on another journey to Tibet. He entered Tibet and was never heard from again.

Janet Lynch-Watson writes of his final trip: "To set out for Tibet in his frail condition was a reckless act. In choosing to go to Tibet it was as if he gathered up his last reserves of strength to make one final sacrifice of love and devotion for his Lord."[16]

Thought to Ponder

Sadhu Sundar Singh much preferred communicating the gospel through his inherited Eastern customs rather than trying to adapt to a Western style of Christian witness. What customs and practices do we use in the West in our mission outreach that might not be essential in spreading the good news about Jesus?

Prayer

Gracious God, I realize that some Christians have had a dramatic conversion like Paul's lightning flash on the Damascus road, whereas other believers have been nurtured in the church and in the home and their experience of faith is more like the coming of the dawn. Lord, may I not be judgmental but willingly accept others whose faith experience might be different from my own. Amen.

THE ROAD TO JOY

Thomas Merton (1915-1968)

I have no greater joy than this,
to hear that my children are
walking in the truth.

3 JOHN 1:4

Thomas Merton, born in Prades, France of artist parents—an American mother and a father from New Zealand—became a Cistercian monk and a prolific spiritual writer. Although he helped many people with his counseling and his writings, he had a lifelong battle with doubt. His regular habit of walking wherever he lived helped him sort out the questions troubling him at the time and ultimately led to "the road to joy."

Merton records his faith journey in his best-selling autobiography, *The Seven Storey Mountain,* published in 1948. In this book, he recalls his early intellectual pilgrimage at Cambridge University in England and later at Columbia University in New York City. Professor Mark Van Doren at Columbia had a strong influence upon him and they later carried on a lively correspondence despite their busy schedules.

Merton became a Roman Catholic in 1938. After teaching a short time at Saint Bonaventure College in Olean, New York, he entered the Trappist monastery, Our Lady of Gethsemani, and was given privileges other monks did not have. For example, Merton was given permission to write and write he did. He published more than forty books in his lifetime. Through his books he made outstanding contributions in the fields of Christian spirituality, peacemaking, race relations, and monastic reform. In particular, he related well to seekers who had problems concerning religious faith. He spoke to their condition out of his own struggles. From Merton's early days in Europe to his last days when he studied Eastern mysticism in countries such as India, China, and Thailand, he always thrilled at opportunities for long walks and mountain climbing. Of course, he did the same in his American setting. When he was teaching at St. Bonaventure, if he wanted to pray, he tended to leave the college buildings and walk in the nearby woods. At

Henri Nouwen on the poor he saw in Latin America: ". . . *men and women walking on the side of the road with heavy burdens on their backs.*"

Henri Nouwen
Walk with Jesus

the Gethsemani Abbey, he walked within the cloister walls, and later, when given permission to be a hermit, he roamed the hills surrounding the abbey. When he went to chapel each day, he had a long hike from his isolated hermitage on the hilltop to the chapel within the cloister walls.

Dominican Thomas Aquinas, who wrote twenty-six books, is estimated to have walked more than nine thousand miles in his intellectual peregrinations across Europe.

Joseph A. Amato
On Foot

Professor Van Doren, his dear friend from Columbia, wrote often. In a letter written in December 1961 he commented, "I shall never forget that day at the retreat, in your class, and on the Abbey walks."[17]

In 1986, long after Merton's accidental death by electrocution while visiting in Thailand, many of his letters were published under the title *The Road to Joy*. The title of the book is taken from something a young girl, Grace Sisson, wrote to him when she was only five years old. She sent him a picture of a house she had drawn. Merton was so delighted with receiving this picture that he wrote a poem, "Grace's House." In the poem, he described everything he saw in the drawing but he ended his letter with the words, "Alas, there is no road to Grace's house."

About five years later, Grace sent Merton another letter containing a drawing of a house but this time with a road leading to the house. She called it "The Road to Joy."[18] Merton thanked her in a reply, writing effusively about the grace of friendship they enjoyed. The little girl symbolized in her drawing of the road something of Merton's own spiritual pilgrimage.

Merton summed up his lifelong quest to understand God in a prayer that expresses the road image:

> My Lord God, I have no idea where I am going. I do not see the road ahead of me. . . . Nor do I really know myself, and the fact that I am following your will does not mean that I am actually doing so. But I believe that the desire to please you does in fact please you.[19]

Merton's friendship with God is best revealed in these simple words— "the road to joy."

Thought to Ponder

Grace, the little girl who corresponded with Thomas Merton, captured the real meaning of our spiritual pilgrimage. It is indeed "the road to joy." What are the specific things that cause you to rejoice today?

Prayer

O God, when I take my daily walk, my feelings overflow with joy as I reflect upon your providence and goodness. You inspire me to walk in the truth as you gradually reveal it to me. I pray in the name of Jesus, who is the truth. Amen.

Until I Couldn't Walk Anymore

Mother Teresa (1910-1997)

Whoever says, "I abide in him,"
ought to walk just as he walked.

1 JOHN 2:6

She calls herself the happiest nun in the world. She belongs to the Sisters of Loreto. She teaches at St. Mary's High School outside of Calcutta, India. She has been teaching for twenty years, and she is basically pleased with this vocation. Then, in 1946, as she travels on a train to Darjeeling for a spiritual retreat, she receives what she terms "a call within a call." She wants to continue as a nun but she now feels God is calling her to go into the slums of Calcutta and work among "the poorest of the poor."

But how can she be certain that she has an authentic call? Perhaps she is deceiving herself. Reflecting on her past she recalls that she is an Albanian by birth, presently a citizen of India and a Catholic nun, she believes she belongs to the whole world, and in her heart she belongs to Jesus.

Born Agnes Gonxha Bojaxhiu in 1910 in Skopje (a city in today's Republic of Macedonia), she grew up in a deeply spiritual family. At the age of twelve she had a desire to be a nun, but during the next six years she lost interest in a religious vocation. When she was eighteen the desire returned and she resolved to leave home and become a missionary. Through contact with Jesuit missionaries who told her of their fascinating work in India, she applied to join the Sisters of Loreto. First, she went to Ireland, the headquarters of the Loreto Sisters. She learned English and in 1929 left for her novitiate in India.

After twenty years of fulfilling teaching, her restlessness compelled her to seek permission from her superiors to undertake a new and challenging type of outreach to the poor. But leaving her comfortable teaching position was even more difficult than leaving her original home.

In 1948, she arrived in the slums of Calcutta, but she was still not sure she had made the right decision. Could she really identify with these people? After pray-

> *Question: "Can you really prayer-walk from your office to the copy machine, from the kitchen to the laundry, from the parking lot to the supermarket?"*
>
> *Answer: "You can if you want to."*
>
> Linus Mundy
> The Complete Guide to
> Prayer-Walking

*Sister Nirmala succeeded
Mother Teresa as leader
of the Missionaries of
Charity in March of 1997.
Undaunted by the prospect
of following in the footsteps
of Mother Teresa, she said,
"I have to walk in my own
shoes. We will continue
as we have been doing."
She has a master's degree
in political science from
an Indian university and
additional training as a
lawyer.*

home.comcast.net/
~motherteresasite/
addresses.html

ing for God's guidance, she formulated a plan to walk through the slums and see what would happen. Balado and Playfoot, in *My Life for the Poor: Mother Teresa of Calcutta,* quote her as saying, "I walked and walked all the time, until I couldn't walk anymore. Then, I understood better the exhaustion of the really poor, always in search of a little food, of medicines, of everything."[20]

That specific walk proved to be pivotal in resolving whether or not to accept the promptings of her heart. Yes, she could live like the people she sought to help. Though she had no shelter, no money, no employment, no security, somehow she believed God would provide. One day in March 1949, a young girl knocked at the door and said, "Mother, I have come to join you." That was the beginning. Soon other young girls arrived to pledge their lives to what God was doing through this tiny nun who came to be known as Mother Teresa.

From those humble beginnings developed a remarkable mission among the poor that eventually spread throughout the world. The pope approved the Missionaries of Charity in 1950. The sisters served Muslim and Hindu people in India and also people of no faith at all. Mother Teresa, in her haunting phrase, saw Christ in his "distressing disguise" in every human being she met.

Today the Missionaries of Charity include more than three thousand sisters working in all parts of the world. They provide hospitals, schools, orphanages, and shelters for the dying in more than five hundred caring centers. The sisters commit themselves to the three monastic vows—poverty, chastity and obedience—and add another, namely service to the poor.

Mother Teresa, known everywhere as the tiny nun in the blue-trimmed, white sari habit, received many prestigious awards including the United States Medal of Freedom, the United Nation's Albert Schweitzer prize, and in 1979, the Nobel Peace Prize. She died on September 5, 1997, on the eve of the funeral of Diana, Princess of Wales. Just a few days before, Mother Teresa had praised Diana for her love and support of the poor.

Mother Teresa once said, "The biggest disease today is not leprosy or tuberculosis, but rather the feeling of being unwanted."[21] Summing up her rationale for such a sacrificial life of service, she stated, "We want to accomplish what a high-level official in our country once said to the sisters, 'It is Christ who is again walking among us doing good.'"[22]

The "good" began that day when a brave nun entered the Calcutta slums and walked and walked until she couldn't walk anymore, and then understood what it meant to be poor.

Thought to Ponder

It was not until Mother Teresa walked among the poor that she really knew how they felt. Call to mind mission work you have done—close to home or far away—and reflect about this event and how it changed your perspective with regard to those less fortunate than you.

Prayer

Merciful God in Jesus, you have taught us how to care. Show me your "call within a call" where I can serve you and others most effectively. Amen.

WALKING THROUGH
THE WORLD UNENCUMBERED

Toyohiko Kagawa (1888-1960)

Though I walk in the midst of trouble,
you preserve me against the wrath of my enemies.

PSALM 138:7

Toyohiko Kagawa, Japanese Christian mystic and social reformer, was born amid wealth, but his boyhood changed drastically in 1892 when his father died. Since Kagawa had been born out of wedlock from a liaison between his father and a concubine, his life with his stepmother now became a time of cruel suffering as she took out her bitterness on young Toyohiko. He was ignored, beaten, and starved for love.

Kagawa found solace in his walks in the nearby bamboo grove, on the sand dunes, and even in the imperial mausoleum. Thus began his love of the natural world that would grow more intense with the passing years.

In 1900, Kagawa entered middle school in Tokushima on the island of Shikoku. Here he came under the influence of two Presbyterian missionaries, Dr. Charles Logan and Dr. Harry Myers, who not only intellectually stimulated the young boy, but also showed him love and acceptance, something he had never known before in his life. As he learned to read the Bible, no words meant more to him than Jesus' words in the Sermon on the Mount. Assigned to memorize this section of the New Testament, when he came to the sixth chapter of Matthew he was overcome with joy at Jesus' teaching about the lilies of the field and God's even greater love for all humankind.

That was the turning point for Kagawa. Although he would still have doubts, from that time on he realized he need not worry about having a Father who would care for him and provide for him forever. A short time later, after further admonitions from Dr. Myers, Kagawa began attending worship, and on February 14, 1904, at the age of fifteen, he was baptized.

Kagawa, an excellent student, had an insatiable appetite for reading books—any book, in any field. After graduating from middle school in 1905, he decided to

On the main island of Honshu, the Japan Alps, also aptly termed the "Roof of Japan," provide excellent scope for hiking.

Robert Strauss
Adventure Trekking

study for the Christian ministry. He first enrolled at the Presbyterian College at Meiji Gakuin in Tokyo. In 1907, however, he moved to Kobe to attend a seminary of the Presbyterian Church (Southern Presbyterian) where he was reunited with his mentor, Dr. Myers, who had joined the faculty.

During his stay in the city of Kobe, Kagawa's love of nature increased and he often wandered on Mount Rokko, overlooking the city. Even when he plunged into mission work in the slums, he often returned to the mountains, taking his bamboo stick to guide him as he hiked for hours up Mount Rokko. Such walking was a source of inner renewal for him.

While studying at the seminary, Kagawa felt called to enter Kobe's overcrowded slums of Shinawa, a place of indescribable poverty, prostitution, crime, and squalor. There he served, sacrificing his own health and placing himself in constant danger. In 1913, he married Haru Shiba, who joined him in his ministry to the poor.

A few years ago I wore shorts up 5000 feet of snow, on a cloudless April day of icy winds, to the . . . rim of Fujiyama—and paid for my stupidity for the rest of the week every time I tried to force red, raw legs into the steaming hot baths that are the only form of ablution in Japanese inns, and which noblesse apparently obliges you to refrain from tempering with cold water. But I remain an unrepentant shorts man.

Colin Fletcher
The Complete Walker, III

The following year Kagawa left Japan and sailed to the United States, where he studied at Princeton Theological Seminary, receiving a bachelor of divinity degree in 1917. Returning to Japan in 1918, he was ordained a minister in the Japanese Presbyterian Church.

Kagawa became a productive author even in his early years of ministry and, in 1920, his autobiographical novel, *Crossing the Death Line,* became a bestseller. He then expanded his social concerns beyond the slums, leading strikers at the Kobe shipyards and organizing the Japan Farmers' Union and the Friends of Jesus Group. Throughout the decades of the 1920s and the 1930s, Kagawa lectured in the United States, Europe, and Asia while still carrying on his ministry at home. As World War II approached, he sought to be a peacemaker, but his attempts were repelled by a militarist government. In the end, he was imprisoned as an annoying pacifist.

Even while in jail, Kagawa found a creative way to walk and to expand his vision of a greater world. In the *Selected Writings of Toyohiko Kagawa,* edited by Keith Beasely-Topliffe, Kagawa is quoted as saying, "My cell was about six feet square, and I could walk about six steps. I walked in the cell for about two miles every day. Thus I could think of my residence as being two miles wide."[23]

In Kagawa's *Meditations,* he frequently uses the image of walking to illustrate the spiritual journey. "In dreaming and waking hours, in sorrow and in laughter, to walk in a world flooded with light, this is a phenomenon expressed only by those who truly know the soul's art."[24]

Again he exults, "The tempestuous rain—I love it! How fine the feeling to walk with head erect, clad in a water-proof, through a raging gale that all but sweeps you off your feet."[25]

And finally, Kagawa sums up his mature faith, one that consists not in clinging to possessions, titles, or other accomplishments, but in something else: "There is nothing more exhilarating than to walk through the world unencumbered . . . stripped to the skin! Stripped to the skin! That is the way to walk."[26]

Thought to Ponder

Kagawa had a hard life in many ways, and yet he trusted God to preserve and protect him as he served others. How has God helped you in the time of trouble?

Prayer

O God, the Rock of Ages, you are my strong fortress in the time of trouble. I cannot serve others on my own. I become overwhelmed with their suffering and misery. Give me the desire and the power to continue to reach out to others in need in the name of Jesus. Amen.

I Could Pray
While I Was Walking

Dorothy Day (1897-1980)

Therefore, I will now allure her,
and bring her into the wilderness,
and speak tenderly to her.

HOSEA 2:14

From her early days in New York City, Dorothy Day had compassion for the poor, but she was not sure how best to go about alleviating their condition. She lacked focus and motivation to enable her to realize her dream. During these days in the metropolitan center she drifted aimlessly, endured a brief marriage, wrote a novel, and continued to search for a purposeful vocation in life. She entered into a common-law marriage with Forster Batterham but they eventually separated when he revolted at Day's desire to have her baby, Tamar, baptized in the church.

Although Day had walked regularly in New York City, it was when she moved to a small fishing cottage on Staten Island that her walking took on a more spiritual tone. God seemed to be preparing her to take a momentous step. The transformation did not come like a lightning flash. Rather, her gallivanting around the waterfront slowly but surely became a gestation period, loosening up previously held rigid thoughts and feeling patterns.

Paul Elie, in his study of Day's life, notes that "she had always been a walker in the city, but during those walks on the beach with Batterham she felt something new and strange: a sudden, strong intuition about the presence of God. . . . To walk in nature was to walk in God's creation."[27]

In her autobiography, *The Long Loneliness,* Day recalls the happy times ambling along the shore where she and Forster walked every day for miles and she began to feel herself opening to the world in new ways. She of course read the great novelists, but she also began to read the Bible again, as well as Thomas à Kempis's *The Imitation of Christ.* Gradually, God seemed to speak

Day's youth in Chicago tenements gave her a taste of life at the bottom rung of society . . . inspired by the books of Upton Sinclair and other social reformers, Day continued visiting low-income areas, finding beauty amid what most considered squalor.

Ira Rifkin, editor
Spiritual Innovators

to her. Once she exclaimed, "I was surprised that I found myself beginning to pray daily. I could not get down on my knees, but I could pray while I was walking."[28] Invariably, if she was sluggish when she began her walk, by the end of her walk she was "filled with exultation.

Day started to attend Mass faithfully on Sunday mornings. The joint walks in the natural world she had with Forster, however, had the opposite effect upon her lover. He would have nothing to do with religion. Finally, Day became pregnant. She was overjoyed; but Forster was not. When her child Tamar was born she desired to have her baptized in the church. Sister Aloysia taught Day the catechism so that she might be grounded in the Christian faith.

In her preparation, Day had the odd notion that she was betraying her long-standing aim to work among the poor. She did not yet realize that Jesus spent his whole life identifying with and serving the poor. She did know the church promoted charity work among the poor but she was more interested in attacking the structures of society and getting at the root causes of poverty.

The man who really gave focus to her life in a ministry of social justice was Peter Maurin. Day returned home once from one of her marches for workers' rights to discover a man who looked like a French peasant sitting in her apartment. Talking with him inspired her in a way no one else had ever done. He saw Christ in others; he was so enthusiastic he convinced Day that she could move mountains on behalf of the poor. When Peter came to New York City, he walked the streets giving everything he had to those who begged from him. Day called him "the Peasant of the Pavements."

Maurin sharpened Day's sense of call by showing her in practical ways what was needed to enable her to fulfill her vision of helping the poor: starting a newspaper for communication, organizing houses of hospitality, and developing farming communities. Above all, Maurin helped her conquer her doubts and he assured her that she was a real Catholic Christian, indeed a woman of faith.[29] Dorothy Day went on to do outstanding work for the poor in her time. Through her leadership in the Catholic Worker Movement, and as a journalist writing *The Catholic Worker* newsletter, she stimulated others to follow her lead. Thomas Merton, Daniel Berrigan, Cesar Chavez, Robert Coles, among many others, were profoundly influenced by her teaching and example. The mature Day combined both an intense piety of constant prayer and worship with deeds of mercy among the

When do pastors have their own Sunday rest? Eugene Peterson says that, when he was a pastor, for many years he and his wife would set aside a special day each week to take a long hike in the woods. *"Monday is my Sabbath.... Before we begin our hike my wife reads a psalm and prays.... We walk leisurely, emptying ourselves, opening ourselves to what is there."*

Eugene Peterson
Working the Angles

impoverished people in urban areas. She also continued to offer a critique of the structures of contemporary society.

Day always remembered when God first spoke to her along the Staten Island beach and prepared her for an extraordinary spiritual and social mission. At a time when she could not kneel in prayer she discovered, "I could pray while I was walking."

Thought to Ponder

Dorothy Day discovered that when she could not pray in a conventional manner, she could pray while she was walking. Share with someone else what prayer-walking means to you.

Prayer

O God, you speak to me in so many different ways, but I hear your voice most clearly when I walk with you in town and in country. There is something about the movement of the body that makes me sensitive to your Spirit and your dynamic presence. Lord, keep me walking, and I shall ever praise your name. Amen.

A Pilgrimage of Trust on Earth

Brother Roger Schutz of Taizé

*All the paths of the Lord are steadfast love and faithfulness,
for those who keep his covenant and his decrees.*

Psalm 25:10

One night in August 1974, a French journalist came across two young people who had just hitchhiked seven hundred miles from Brittany to come to the village of Taizé, so tiny it was not even marked on many maps in France. He saw in this rain-drenched couple, walking the last leg of their journey, a passionate desire for real love and justice.

The couple had come to the right place. Ever since the 1940s people young and old, but mostly young, had come by plane, bus, car, or simply on foot to this tiny village of Taizé. Here in this humble place of worship Roger Schutz and his brother monks welcomed them with open arms. After sharing a unique fellowship of reconciliation, the participants returned to their respective homes to serve among the dispossessed and disillusioned people on their own doorstep.

Who was Roger Schutz? Born in 1915 in Provence, near Neuchatel in the French-speaking part of Switzerland, he was raised by devout parents. His father was a Reformed pastor and his mother also shared the Reformed faith. His maternal grandmother, however, was Roman Catholic. From an early age, Roger came under the influence of parents and a grandmother who respected each other's faith. They provided the foundation for the ecumenical spirit he exhibited throughout his life.

As a young man, Roger thought of becoming a writer but he soon changed his mind when editors wanted him to alter his thoughts. Instead, in 1937, he began to study theology in Lausanne and later in Strasbourg. Gradually he began dreaming of finding a house where he and a few others could confine themselves to prayer, silence, fellowship, and service among the poor. When France was defeated and occupied by German forces near the beginning of World War II, he saw that country as an ideal location to serve among a downtrodden people.

*Walking is not only good for
our bodies and minds, but
it is soul food. And let us
not forget that older people
walk to the sunrise.*

Richard L. Morgan
No Wrinkles on the Soul

Roger traveled through France looking for a place to start his work. His biographer, J. L. G. Balado, explains what happened one day:

> Walking through the narrow streets of the ancient [Cluny], Roger suddenly saw a paper fixed on a door: "House for sale in Taizé." He went and visited an old woman who had the keys to the house in Taizé, and she pleaded with him, "Stay here with us: we are poor, so isolated and the times are bad."[30]

Roger returned to Switzerland and talked the plans over with his friends. Later, he returned to Cluny and told the owner he wanted to buy the house in Taizé. This house became a safe place for refugees fleeing the Nazis during the war. Not a few of the refugees were Jews.

After World War II ended, Roger returned to his theological studies in Switzerland. While he was there, he gathered around him a few committed men who shared his vision of a reconciling community. They moved to Taizé and, despite post-war austerity, they met three times a day for prayer and farmed the fields as best they could.

The brothers who joined Roger's community took the historic monastic vows of poverty, chastity, and obedience. When at Taizé, the brothers dressed in simple white robes, and when they labored in town or in the countryside they wore regular work clothes. The music at Taizé with its distinctive chants, was well received by the youth and was carried back by them to churches all over the world.

In time, Brother Roger developed his "Rule of Taizé," a simple set of instructions that guided this reconciling community. At the heart of the rule was the charge to each new member: "Henceforth walk in the steps of Christ. Do not be anxious about tomorrow. Seek first God's kingdom and his justice."[31]

Through the years, thousands and thousands of pilgrims came to Taizé for a taste of a simple but powerful worship experience, and then they were sent back to their homes to be reconcilers among their own people. Brother Roger, as well as the other brothers, traveled throughout the world bearing witness and serving among the urban and rural poor.

During a 1982 visit to Lebanon, Brother Roger set forth in a circular letter a new concept called "A Pilgrimage of Trust on Earth." He proposed that, instead of coming to Taizé, people young and old come together in their own locale as pilgrims of peace, bearers of reconciliation in the church and of trust on earth. Each year Roger sent out an open letter to all such sojourners encouraging them to be involved in their neighborhoods, demonstrating the Taizé experience on every continent.

Brother Roger has won awards, including the coveted Templeton Prize (in 1974), the UNESCO Prize for Peace Education (in 1988) and the international "Karlspries" for his contribution to the reconstruction of Europe (in 1989).

John Woodbridge
More Than Conquerors

On August 16, 2005, ninety-year-old Roger joined a congregation of 2,500 people for a prayer service in Taizé. In the midst of the service a deranged thirty-six-year-old Romanian woman suddenly leaped out of the crowd and stabbed Brother Roger in the throat three times. Within minutes he was dead.

The spirit of Taizé, however, did not die with him but continues to our present day. When Pope John XXIII recalled his visit to Taizé he sighed, "Ah Taizé, that little springtime!" In Roger's mind it was always springtime because, as he said repeatedly, "I trust the new generations. . . . I trust the young."[32]

Thought to Ponder

Brother Roger Schutz of Taizé had the vision of bringing together Christians, young people in particular, from all over the world to engage in a covenant of reconciliation. He beautifully combined vibrant worship with Christian witness and social action. What areas of life in your own time and place are in most urgent need of the reconciling spirit?

Prayer

Gracious Lord, grant me an ecumenical vision so that I can see your church in all its fullness. May I be committed to a ministry of reconciliation not only within my own church family but in the wider church, too. This intercession I make in the name of Jesus who prayed that we all might be one. Amen.

PROPHETS
&
SOCIAL REFORMERS

Walking in a Human Jungle

William Booth (1829-1912)

A voice cries out:
"In the wilderness prepare the way of the LORD,
make straight in the desert a highway for our God."

ISAIAH 40:3

One July night in 1865, she waited patiently in her comfortable West London home for her husband to come home. He had left the house that day and walked to East London in search of a mission. He was a restless evangelistic preacher with enormous energy but without a single focus. He wanted to serve the poor, to show them a better life, the abundant life he had found in Christ. As his biographer, William Collier, puts it: "For all the crusading years of his life, he had sought a human jungle. Now he walked in its midst."[1]

That night he witnessed poverty such as he had never seen before in his life. East London had more than 500,000 people jammed together in the most inhospitable conditions of poverty, filth, and crime. The thirty-six-year-old William Booth desperately wanted to help people who had been forgotten or shunned by others. Finally, he returned home that steamy night close to midnight. No sooner had he entered the house than he exclaimed to his wife, "Darling, I've found my Destiny."[2] She could not help but wonder what that might mean for her and her young children.

Growing up in Nottingham, William Booth knew the pangs of poverty, especially when he was apprenticed at an early age to work in a pawnbroker's shop where the poor traded their meager possessions for loans at interest. Although he attended the Church of England services when he was young, he did not receive much spiritual nourishment. Soon he was attracted to the more vibrant Methodist meetings where he was converted at the age of fifteen.

As a young man, he moved to London where he worked as a pawnbroker and preached on the side. While working in London, he met the remarkable Catherine Mumford and they fell in love. About this time, Booth was assigned to a small Methodist circuit at Spaulding

Moments after the horrific shootings at Virginia Tech (USA), Salvation Army emergency disaster services personnel were at the college offering comfort and support.

www.salvationarmy.org

in Lincolnshire. This particular assignment meant that he was separated for a while from Catherine; however, by 1855, they were married and together began a powerful Christian ministry.

William would not be confined to his circuit responsibilities. Increasingly, he held revivals in surrounding towns with huge success. The Methodist officials criticized him for not being an observant minister. At last in 1861, he resigned from his position and, with no prospects of financial security for his wife and four young children, he launched out on an uncertain future.

He and his family returned to London and he preached wherever people would listen. He even went into the notorious slums of East London where no else wanted to go. It was here in this "human jungle" that he found his call on that fateful night, the cause that henceforth would define his life.

East London was an exceedingly difficult mission field even for the commanding gifts and energy of William Booth. He soon became the leader of what was called the East London Revival Society, later called The Christian Mission. The poor began to respond to his fervent evangelical message. Before long Booth employed military imagery to promote his revivals and, in 1878, his followers became known as the Salvation Army. Their uniforms, band instruments, and the habit of holding meetings on city street corners soon made them a target of ridicule for some, but for others they were the conveyers of salvation and healing.

The eighteen thousand Indians were forced to march from their homes in Alabama, Tennessee, Georgia, and North Carolina to Oklahoma, then Indian Territory, in the heart of winter. Many had to walk, and their shoeless feet left tracks of blood on the earth and in the snow. Four thousand Cherokee, mostly children and old people, died along that route which has become known as the Trail of Tears.

Jerry Ellis
Walking the Trail

William became the general of this "army" with absolute control. His whole family was involved in the mission in one way or another. His wife, Catherine, was a powerful preacher in her own right. Later, his daughter Evangeline and his son William became generals too.

Today, the Salvation Army has more than two million officers and members serving throughout the world. They combine an unabashed evangelical message with a unique form of practical social service. The have founded hospitals, schools, and other rehabilitation homes. No current religious organization is held in such high respect by believers and by persons with no religious faith at all.

The turning point for William Booth was that late night walk through the streets of East London. That walk convinced him that God was demonstrating for him where he should invest the rest of his life. He was called to work among the impoverished people no one else seemed to be concerned about at that time. He found his "human jungle" and his reason for being.

Thought to Ponder

William Booth was not satisfied to serve God in an imprecise way. He wanted to receive a specific call to service. In making personal decisions, which resources do you depend upon the most: the Bible, the church, or the Holy Spirit speaking to you directly? Or is it a combination of all three? Explain the reasons for your choice.

Prayer

God of Abraham, Isaac, and Jacob, you have raised up prophets in every generation to speak to your people. Grant me patience as I await your call to personal service in my own day. Amen.

MARCHING IN THE NAME OF GOD

Mohandas Gandhi (1869-1948)

*And what does the LORD require of you
but to do justice, and to love kindness,
and to walk humbly with your God.*

MICAH 6:8

Mohandas Gandhi made a habit of daily walking in his early years. As a mature man he could out-walk anyone. In time, his practice of regular walking would be transformed into a symbol for gaining independence for his Indian people through nonviolent means. His example of passive resistance has profoundly influenced religious and social reformers who came after him.

Gandhi was born in Porbandar, India, in 1869. When he was only thirteen years old his parents arranged a marriage with a girl his same age. They eventually had four children. As a promising young man he was sent to England to study law. When he returned to India as a barrister, however, he could not find suitable employment. Therefore, in 1893, Gandhi decided to go to South Africa. Even though he was a British subject, he suffered discrimination in South Africa because he was an Indian. He originally planned to stay in this country only one year, but in fact he stayed twenty-one years, with occasional visits to India.

He developed the concept of *satyagraha* or "soul force"[3] whereby, through peaceful civil disobedience, he pressed his case for the humane treatment of Indians. He was deeply influenced by the teachings of Jesus, in particular the Sermon on the Mount. Most of the Christians he met in South Africa, however, did not convince him he should become a member of the church.

Fitness is not a commodity to be stored, rather a condition to be renewed on a daily basis. Have you had your walk today?

Bonnie Stein
Welcome to Racewalking

In 1914, Gandhi returned to India and soon became a leader of the Indian Nationalist Party. He led numerous peaceful protests on behalf of his people. Finally, in 1947, England granted India its political freedom. However, Gandhi was unhappy with the partition of the population of India that resulted in Hindu adherents living in India itself and Muslim believers being located

in Pakistan. He often fasted to bring attention to the values he held dearly. In 1948, while on his way to a prayer meeting, Gandhi was killed by a Hindu zealot.

Of all of Gandhi's memorable walks for social justice, his 1930 trek across India on foot to protest a salt tax on his people became pivotal in his quest for Indian independence. On March 2, 1930, Gandhi drew up a letter listing eleven principal grievances he felt would lead to independence—if England accepted them. However, if the English authorities did not respond positively, he was prepared to lead a peaceful march against the salt tax that afflicted especially the poor people of the land.

Mohandas Karamchand Gandhi (Mahatma is an honorific meaning 'great soul') was raised steeped in Hinduism and Jainism, giving him an appreciation for ahimsa (non-injury for all living beings), vegetarianism, and fasting.

Ira Rifkin, editor
Spiritual Innovators

On March 12, 1930, Gandhi, along with seventy-eight followers, began a 240-mile march to the sea at Dandi. His group included not only Hindu religionists but also two Muslims and one Christian. Gandhi, with his iron-tipped bamboo walking staff, led the march with firm assurance. Each day he led prayer meetings, and he engaged in spinning wool for an hour. The sight of this sixty-nine-year-old man at the head of his motley group somehow attracted others who saw him defying the might of the British Empire. By the time he and his followers had reached Dandi on the sea coast, his band had expanded into the thousands. Throughout the long journey Gandhi spurred on the people with the ringing cry, "We are marching in the name of God."[4]

Later in Gandhi's life, Louis Fischer, the biographer, visited him. The two of them went for long walks each day. They talked as they ambled along the way. After a half hour Fischer became tired and he was ready for a rest, but Gandhi continued to talk and seemingly was not exhausted at all. He was seventy-three years old.[5]

Gandhi was an earnest walker to the end of his days, but no walk he ever undertook had more far-reaching consequences than the 1930 march to the sea protesting the salt tax. This procession galvanized his people and ultimately led them on the road to political independence.

Thought to Ponder

Gandhi single-handedly motivated his people to seek political independence for India through nonviolent means. How might you effect social change in your own community? Is passive resistance a viable option for you? Why or why not?

Prayer

O God of the nations, you work among people representing every background, nation and race whenever they are willing to walk humbly in your way. Deepen my own convictions so that I may be willing to march for a worthwhile cause in your name. Amen.

I'm Bound for the Promised Land

Harriet Tubman (1822-1913)

*For the LORD will be your confidence
and will keep your foot from being caught.*

PROVERBS 3:26

Harriet Tubman walked to freedom, escaping slavery in Maryland's Eastern Shore; and then she marched right back over and over again, at great risk to her own life, to rescue scores of others.

Born Araminta "Minty" Ross in 1822, she changed her name to Harriet Tubman when she married John Tubman in 1844. She grew up on a slave plantation owned by Anthony Thompson. She was hired out to other planters as a child. Sometime between 1834 and 1836, she was struck accidentally in the head by a heavy iron weight thrown mistakenly by an overseer at someone else for misbehaving. For the rest of her life she suffered seizures due to this injury.

It is not certain when she came under the influence of evangelical Christianity but sometime before her marriage she was profoundly stirred by black preachers, white Methodist services, and camp meetings. She embraced a fervent Christian faith, and along with her faith an inner conviction that God was going to liberate her and call her to be the means of freeing other slaves.

In 1849, when her master's widow had to sell slaves to pay debts, Harriet decided that now was the time to seek her freedom. Though her husband was reluctant to go, Harriet left anyway, hurrying through the Maryland woods under cover of darkness until she crossed over the Pennsylvania border and found freedom in Philadelphia. The journey was difficult and dangerous, but what really set Harriet apart from others was her determination to go back and attempt to rescue as many of her own family and friends who were willing to take the risk. Before long she earned the nickname "Moses" because she led so many slaves out of the Eastern Shore region of Maryland to the northern states and eventually to Canada.

In 1989 Jerry Ellis, a Cherokee descendent, decided to walk the Trail of Tears his ancestors were forced to march in the dead of winter in 1838. He completed the nine hundred miles and exclaimed: *"I . . . entered into an odyssey that will feed me for the rest of my life."*

Jerry Ellis
Walking the Trail

Harriet's recent biographer, Kate Clifford Larson, writes that the forests in the Eastern Shore area were littered with seedpods of the sweet gum tree. These spiny, prickly burrs pierced the feet of the runaway slaves. The slaves could not cry out when hurt since that might lead to their capture by the pursuing slave owners. Larson comments, "How ironic that the sweet gum would be so cruel."[6]

Harriet usually made her escape on a Saturday since there would be no Sunday papers to warn the public that slaves had escaped. She also cleverly planned most of her escapes during the winters when the nights were long, although she occasionally made trips in the warmer weather as well. She moved swiftly through the night hours using the North Star to guide her to safety. When she left the Maryland plantation for the first time, she sang the spiritual "I'm bound for the promised land."[7] In fact, Tubman frequently sang spirituals with coded messages to warn escapees under her care of danger nearby.

Harriet settled in St. Catherines, Ontario, Canada. From that base of operations, she made her walking forays into the Maryland countryside. Shortly after the Fugitive Slave Act was passed in 1850, she brought back her niece, Kessiah, and her two children. The next year she returned to lead her brother Moses and several other slaves to freedom. When she asked her husband to join them, he refused to go. He had remarried in the meantime and was content to stay where he was. Still later, Harriet returned to bring three other brothers to safety, as well as other relatives and friends.

In 1859, Harriet moved to Fleming, New York, where she bought property. By this time she had become famous for her unique role in the Underground Railroad. She spoke widely to enthusiastic crowds. She could not read or write, but she was a dramatic storyteller. A woman small in stature, she possessed a beautiful singing voice and an astounding memory, demonstrated in the way she quoted from the Bible throughout her talks.

In 1861, when the Civil War began, she became a cook, a nurse, and even a spy for the Union Army in South Carolina. In 1863, she became the first woman to lead an armed raid under the command of Colonel James Montgomery when Union troops defeated Confederate forces and freed more than seven hundred slaves. After the war ended, she was seriously injured when a racist conductor violently threw her off a passenger train.

In 1869, Harriet married Nelson Davis. She continued to farm her property and to help her husband

> *"Walking" in Latino and African-American circles today stands as a metaphor for what kind of witness one gives in one's everyday life.... For Latinos and African-Americans, a "walking gospel" is one that eschews the air and armchair for the streets, and incarnates the Christian faith in the world, connecting the gospel to public issues.*
>
> Leonard Sweet
> The Jesus Prescription
> for a Healthy Life

with his brick-making business. Subsequently, she became active in the suffrage movement. She had a sense of the future, and she bought a twenty-five acre plot of land next to her own property to establish a home for elderly black people. In 1903, she transferred this property to the AME Zion Church. Harriet Tubman died in 1913 and is buried in Auburn, New York. Never has there been a more courageous walker who sacrificed herself time and time again to lead fellow slaves to the "promised land" of freedom. She truly was a "Moses" to her people.

Thought to Ponder

Harriet Tubman, like the biblical Moses, led many of her fellow slaves out of bondage. What do you think were the major sources of inspiration that enabled this remarkable woman to undertake such dangerous ventures?

Prayer

Redeeming God, grant me the courage to do something daring in my own time. Fortify me with the confidence that if I am doing your will I will not be caught in a trap but will find a way to accomplish my aim. Amen.

No Orthodoxy in Walking

George Macaulay Trevelyan (1876-1962)

Vindicate me, O Lord,
for I have walked in my integrity.

Psalm 26:1

George Macaulay Trevelyan, one of England's greatest historians, was an enthusiastic walker throughout his adulthood. Even when he was in his seventies he was apt to ask unsuspecting guests to go for "short strolls" after dinner, strolls that frequently turned out to be thirty-mile hikes.

Trevelyan grew up in the rugged but beautiful Northumberland County in northeastern England. Even though his education and work took him to Cambridge, London, and other urban centers, he always returned to the Northumberland countryside for what he called "spiritual values." He belonged to the English aristocracy. His father, Sir George Otto Trevelyan, was active in the Liberal government of William Gladstone and did historical writing of his own. George's great uncle, Lord Macaulay, was an influential figure in nineteenth-century England.

Trevelyan studied at Harrow and at Trinity College, Cambridge. He earned a fellowship at Trinity in 1898, which enabled him to turn his dissertation into a book, *England in the Age of Wycliffe* (1889). Nonetheless, in 1903, he resigned his fellowship, married Jane Penrose Ward, and ventured forth away from the academic world to explore his own style of historical writing.

Trevelyan's burden, one that greatly troubled his heart, was the relentless industrialization of England during the twentieth century. Though he recognized the positive side of this development, he felt that too much was lost for people in all strata of society. He believed that the poor especially suffered from the blight of overcrowded and dismal slums in the cities. Therefore, Trevelyan spent most of his adult life extolling the virtues of the countryside. He did so by taking long walks year after year. He was also a fervent advocate for legislation that would protect the countryside for all people. He was a consistent supporter of The National Trust that sought to preserve precious landmarks of

How far can I expect to walk in a day? For most kinds of walking, the question is wrongly put. Except along flat, straight roads, miles are just about meaningless. Hours are what count.

Colin Fletcher
The Complete Walker, III

English heritage and large sections of rural area from being used for housing and industrial development.

Trevelyan enjoyed tramping long distances in the sparsely populated regions of his beloved land. There are few places in Great Britain he did not walk. Of course, he knew the hills and moors of Northumberland like no one else. He also traveled on foot throughout Scotland and he walked around the southern coast of Devon and Cornwall several times. Biographer David Cannadine comments on one of his treks:

> On one occasion he went on a walking tour to the West Country with Bertrand Russell, himself no faint heart, who made Trevelyan promise to be content with a mere twenty-five miles a day. "He kept his promise," Russell later recorded, "until the last day. Then he left me, saying now he must have a little walking."[8]

Trevelyan's philosophy of walking appears most clearly in his essay "Walking." He begins by stating: "I have two doctors, my left leg and my right. When body and mind are out of gear . . . I know that I shall only need to call in my doctors and I shall be well again."[9] He goes on to celebrate the joy of walking in England and in Italy.

He acknowledges that there are many different types of walkers. Some he calls "road walkers" who prefer the open road. He lists Robert Louis Stevenson as an outstanding road walker. These devotees want to cover as much ground as possible. Others he labels "climbers" or "scramblers." They are the ones who love to climb or scramble up the mountainside. They are not content just to walk on the open road. They want to know the texture of the rocks, the smell of the moss, and the throb of the high places.

But for Trevelyan, cross-country walking was closest to his heart. That is why he resented the fencing in of so much open land and the penetration of industry into rural areas. He was convinced that there is something intrinsically precious about the countryside. Most of all he enjoyed walking by himself. Physical exercise was important to him, but even more important was what long-distance walking did for his soul. He found what he called "spiritual values" in such walking. No matter what the weather might be, he relished his daily hike, and he frequently continued walking into the twilight hours. He contended that after a day's walking, everything, including eating and reading, has "twice its usual value."[10]

Subsidize your walking group: *"Here's a nutty idea. While walking, keep an eye out for valuables along the road. Okay, this really won't help a club get going, but four-time Olympic racewalker Carl Schueler has accumulated almost an entire metric socket set from the roadside, and figures he can send his daughter to college on collected spare-change thanks to his eagle eye. (Well, almost.) Maybe you can help underwrite the club picnic with what you find."*

Mark Fenton and David Bassett Jr.
Pedometer Walking

Although hiking amid the heather and the gorse was his favorite way of walking, he did not despise other forms of traveling on foot. He concludes his essay by noting, "There is no orthodoxy in Walking. It is a land of many paths and no-paths, wherever one goes his own way is right."[11]

Thought to Ponder

George Macaulay Trevelyan was indeed a man who walked with integrity. He was a strong advocate for walking no matter what style someone might choose. What is your favorite kind of walking? Why do you say so?

Prayer

God of creation, what a magnificent world you have given us! May I never take for granted the beauty that surrounds me. Assist me, Lord, that I may walk in integrity and appreciate your whole creation. Amen.

It Is the Perfect
Aesthetic Experience

Bob Marshall (1901-1939)

*When my spirit is faint,
you know the way.*

PSALM 142:3

What can you say about a young man who hiked thirty-five miles one day, and then, after supper, decided to walk five miles more so that he could round out his average of walking forty miles a day? Surely, he was obsessive about walking, but his passion would one day motivate him to become one of America's leading conservationists in the twentieth century. Today, more than five million acres of Montana wilderness that he fought to protect is appropriately named after him—Bob Marshall Country.

Although Bob Marshall's great contribution was preserving the natural environment in the West, his story actually began in the East. Marshall's father, a constitutional lawyer, fought for minorities, including his own Jewish people, and he argued strenuously for the conservation of the undeveloped areas of the Adirondacks and the Catskills in the state of New York. His son, Bob, came to love the natural world of this New York wilderness. In 1920, Marshall enrolled in the New York State School of Forestry at Syracuse University, where he excelled in scholarship.

The following summer, Marshall and his brother George decided to climb all the mountains in the Adirondacks that were four-thousand feet or higher. He calculated that forty-two mountains fit into this category. Marshall gained tremendous satisfaction in rating things. He also documented more than ninety-four lakes and ponds in the wilderness area. In 1924, he graduated fourth in his class and scored first in a national Civil Service test for foresters.

Marshall viewed the wilds as a place of recreation and inspiration. Like Thoreau, he could not understand how anyone could live indefinitely in the city without

Exploring the world on foot invites you to extend your interests through looking to the sky and to the earth, learning the ways of a rockhound, stargazer, botanist, wildlife enthusiast, or any of the many other faces of the jigsaw that is life on this planet.

Robert Strauss
Adventure Trekking

doing serious harm to their inner being. After obtaining a master's degree from Harvard University, he headed to the Northern Rocky Mountain Forest and Range Experimental Station in Missoula, Montana. He spent three years in this region, and the Marshall legend began. He wore old, tattered clothes wherever he went. He continued his penchant for rating everything and, of course, he walked his customary forty miles a day or more. He deemed himself a good cook, but in his early attempts his fellow adventurers claimed that even his hard-boiled eggs were inedible.

Already his heart was giving signs of weakening; nevertheless, Marshall continued his forty-mile hikes each day in the Bitteroots, Flatheads, Missions, Cascades, and Selkirks. Many of these hikes reached fifty miles a day. He would return home exhausted, but he cherished the wilderness and exclaimed, "It is the perfect aesthetic experience."[12]

Elaborating on this sentiment in a *Nature* article in 1937, he wrote:

> It is a vast panorama, full of height and depth and flowing color, on a scale so overwhelming as to wipe out the ordinary meaning of dimensions. It is the song of the hermit thrush at twilight. It is the unique odor of balsams and of freshly turned humus. It is the feel of spruce needles underfoot.[13]

From 1928 to 1930, Marshall studied at Johns Hopkins University and received his doctorate in plant physiology. In 1931, he left for Alaska where he spent thirteen months exploring the Koyukuk River. Impressed by the inhabitants of the area, on his return East he wrote his most influential book, *Artic Village,* a valuable sociological study of a wilderness settlement.

More and more, Marshall became convinced that America's wilderness was being threatened by developers and loggers. He sought to organize people to fight for the freedom of the rugged frontier. To him, it was not just a regional problem but a national one. He contacted Gifford Pinchot and President Franklin D. Roosevelt, known to be sympathetic toward conservation, and urged them to use their power and authority to protect the wilderness. Marshall also had compassion for Native Americans in the West and he did everything he could to improve life on the reservations

In 1937, Marshall became sick, and he became increasingly irritable toward people who did not share his enthusiasm for the wilds. As might be expected, the more vocal he became the more vested interests sought to curtail his ecological crusade.

In the summers of 1938 and 1939, Marshall returned to Alaska to explore the peaks in the Brooks Range. He was a man who seemingly could not rest

A year after Bob Marshall's death in 1939 a wilderness was created in Montana in his honor. He wanted to see wildernesses where people could travel for two weeks without crossing a road. The 1,009,000-acre Bob Marshall Wilderness is known to aficionados as "The Bob."

gorp.away.com

despite his failing health. He returned East a short time after the Alaska trip. While traveling on a train from Washington, D.C., to New York City, he died in his sleep at the age of thirty-nine.

The Wilderness Society received a third of Marshall's estate, a significant $500,000, to help bring to fruition his lifetime goals. Sherry Devlin preserves for us the following poignant words written by Marshall the year before his death:

> We're all young enough that we'll probably meet many defeats in the next 50 years. It's even conceivable that when we die we still will not have won the fight. But win or lose, it will be grand fun fighting and knowing that whatever we do in the right direction will help eventual victory.[14]

Thought to Ponder

Bob Marshall's heart was always in the great American wilderness, and though he died in the prime of his life, he left a legacy of some of the most beautiful land in our nation. What specific things have you learned from this vignette that might inspire you to be a leader in present-day efforts to preserve the natural environment?

Prayer

O God of the Big Sky Country and Lord of the universe, grant me a vision of land still to be explored. Move me out of my familiar setting so that my heart might throb at the sights and sounds of the wild. I may grow faint at times, but I trust you know the way. Amen.

Wanderer with a Purpose

Peace Pilgrim (d. 1981)

How beautiful upon the mountains
are the feet of the messenger
who announces peace,
who brings good news,
who announces salvation,
who says to Zion, "Your God reigns."

Isaiah 52:7

The silver-haired woman dressed in slacks and a blue shirt with "Peace Pilgrim" printed on the front of her tunic and "25,000 Miles on Foot for Peace" printed on the back gathers a crowd as she walks across America. She is a strange sight to many people, but once a person meets her, he or she inevitably goes away with a fresh sense of inner peace and a passion for peace in the world.

What little we know about this remarkable woman comes from a book, *Peace Pilgrim: Her Life and Work in Her Own Words,* compiled by some of her friends. Born in the eastern United States near the beginning of the twentieth century, she lived her early life on a small farm. She lived in a modest house, but eventually she prospered and gained both money and possessions. Her self-centered life, however, became meaningless and she sought something better.

She describes how her quest came to fruition during one of her earlier walks:

> I walked all one night through the woods. I came to a moonlight glade and prayed. I felt a complete willingness, without any reservations, to give my life—to dedicate my life—to service. "Please use me!" I prayed to God. And a great peace came over me.[15]

Peace Pilgrim began to prepare herself for a life of service but at that juncture in her journey she did not know what form the service would take. She sought to develop a right attitude toward life and go below the surface of life where truth was to be found. She proceeded to bring her goals in harmony with the laws that govern the universe. Then she looked for a special place in

God's plan as she simplified her life and brought herself down to what she called her *need* level.

Once again, the walking image helped her find her way. Climbing a hill, she sat down in a place overlooking rural New England. She described her dream in this manner:

> I saw a map of the United States with the large cities marked—and it was as though someone had taken a colored crayon and marked a zigzag line across, coast to coast and border to border, from Los Angeles to New York City. I knew what I was to do: and that was a vision of my first year's pilgrimage route in 1953.[16]

She had entered "a new and wonderful world" and from now on her life would be blessed with a clear purpose. In 1953, she went forth as a pilgrim with no money, only the clothes on her back. She fasted until someone gave her food. She found shelter wherever she could, often simply resting at night in the open air. She not only believed in the Golden Rule—do unto others, as you would have them do unto you—she lived it. She loved everyone she met. If someone would listen, she told that person how to find inner peace. Soon she was invited to speak in schools, in churches, and to other organized groups. She had trying times too. For example, somewhere between El Paso and Dallas, Texas, she was arrested for vagrancy. She was interrogated by the F.B.I., and when they took her picture in the jail, she was the only one smiling. They released her promptly.

At first, she walked along the main highways, but in time she turned to the country roads where she discovered she could meet more people. She usually averaged about twenty-five miles walking each day, but she walked as many as fifty miles in one day when no shelter was available. She hiked on very cold nights to keep warm and if the day was extremely hot she ambled along at night to avoid the heat.

She once stated:

> How many steps do Americans take?
>
> *"33 percent take less than 5,000 steps per day. 29 percent take 5,001 to 7,500 steps per day. 22 percent take 7,501 to 10,000 steps per day. 16 percent take more than 10,000 steps per day."*
>
> Mark Fenton and
> David Bassett Jr.
> Pedometer Walking

> When I started out on my pilgrimage, I was using walking for two purposes at that time. One was to contact people, and I still use it for that purpose today. But the other was as a prayer discipline, to keep me concentrating on my prayer for peace. And after a few years I discovered something. I discovered that I no longer needed the prayer discipline. I pray without ceasing now.[17]

Wherever possible she spoke to people about peace in the world. She firmly believed that war was contrary to both God's will and common sense and she summoned everyone to be willing to pay the price for peace. She realized how easy governments persuade people to go to war and she did not believe the end justified the means. On the contrary, according to her spiritual values, the means determined the end, and further, only a good means can really attain a good end.

Peace Pilgrim set a singular example for her own generation and for future generations. She died in a tragic head-on collision as she was being driven to a speaking engagement near Knox, Indiana, on July 7, 1981. As she would have said, it would be "the glorious transition to a freer life."[18]

Throughout her endless walking, Peace Pilgrim never thought she was protesting something but rather that she was making a witness for peace and harmonious living.

Thought to Ponder

Peace Pilgrim was often ridiculed for her bold witness for peace. Have you ever endured criticism for taking a stand? How did you handle it? What resources did you rely on?

Prayer

God of peace, I pray for the courage to walk for a cause despite the taunts of others. As one of Jesus' disciples, may I be a peacemaker in word and deed. Amen.

"Little Old Lady in Tennies"
"Peace Pilgrim Marches on . . . and on . . ."
Headlines from *Los Angeles Times*
December 3, 1973

WALKING THE STREETS IN DIGNITY

Martin Luther King Jr. (1929-1968)

I am about to do a new thing; now it springs forth,
do you not perceive it?
I will make a way in the wilderness
and rivers in the desert.

ISAIAH 43:19

As a young boy Martin Luther King Jr. wanted to learn a few "big" words so that he could preach like his namesake father who was pastor of the prominent Ebenezer Baptist Church in Atlanta, Georgia. King did learn a few big words, but more importantly, he learned how to convey his message in the extremely effective form of nonviolent demonstrations.

King was born in a middle-class black neighborhood in Atlanta. A precocious student, he entered Morehouse College in Atlanta at the age of fifteen. He did his theological education at Crozer Theological Seminary in Chester, Pennsylvania, and later he gained a Ph.D. in theology at Boston University. While studying in Boston he met Coretta Scott of Marion, Alabama, who was preparing for a career in music. They were married before they returned to the South where Martin was called to be the pastor of the Dexter Avenue Baptist Church in Montgomery, Alabama.

Little did the young couple know that they were about to be caught up in one of the major controversies of their day. The following year, in 1955, Rosa Parks was arrested for refusing to give up her seat and go to the back of the bus when more white people came on her particular bus. For a long time the black community of Montgomery had been unhappy about segregation on buses but no one did anything about it. Now that Rosa Parks had sharpened the issue, black leaders throughout the city came to the conclusion that all black citizens should boycott the buses—but they needed a commander to solidify their protest.

King had been in the city for only a year, focusing on his own pastoral ministry. Nonetheless, the leaders of the black community prevailed upon him to give them motivation and direction. He accepted the responsibility

> *Dr. King's favorite hymn was "Precious Lord, Take My Hand," written by Thomas A. Dorsey in 1932, when his wife and baby boy died suddenly and he sought comfort and hope from his Lord.*
>
> *Robert J. Morgan*
> Then Sings My Soul

and told them he would only advocate nonviolent action, a method he had learned through the study of Jesus' Sermon on the Mount and the practice of Mohandas Gandhi in India.

For more than a year, the black people of Montgomery boycotted the buses. They would not ride in them no matter how far away they lived from their work. They walked in all kinds of weather. They resolved to somehow break the law of segregation that had held them in bondage for so many years. King eloquently summed up their spirit when he wrote in his book *Strength to Love*, "The Negro community of Montgomery . . . came to see that it was ultimately more honorable to walk the streets in dignity than to ride the buses in humiliation."[19]

In 1956, the black people of Montgomery were jubilant when the Supreme Court of the United States struck down the old segregation law regarding public buses. The persistence of these intrepid people had won the battle. In 1957, the Southern Christian Leadership Conference (SCLC) was organized based on King's philosophy of nonviolent action to combat prejudice and discrimination. Soon King and the SCLC gained a national reputation, and the modern civil rights movement came into being.

In 1960, King and his family moved to Atlanta and he became co-pastor with his father of Ebenezer Baptist Church. On August 28, 1963, more than two-hundred thousand people marched and gathered in front of the Lincoln Memorial in Washington, D.C., to encourage President John F. Kennedy to support much-needed civil rights legislation. The march reached its climax with King's magnificent "I Have a Dream" address. King explained the rationale for his freedom marches in another book, *A Testament of Hope,* by stating, "When marches are carefully organized around well-defined issues, they represent the power which Victor Hugo phrased as the most powerful force in the world, 'an idea whose time has come.' Marching feet announce that time has come for a given idea."[20]

Rabbi Abraham Heschel joins Martin Luther King Jr. for the march on Selma, Alabama: *"The white-bearded Heschel had just led a march in New York to FBI headquarters protesting brutality against Selma protesters. Now, in Selma, he wrote in his diary that 'I felt a sense of the Holy in what I was doing.' He felt 'as though my legs were praying.'"*

Stewart Burns
To the Mountaintop

King further declared that if meaningful results were to take place it was necessary that marches extend over a period of sufficient time, perhaps thirty or forty days. These marches needed to be of maximum size so that the resistant powers would take notice. That is to say, "they must demand the attention of the press, for it is the press which interprets the issue to the community at large and thereby sets in motion the machinery for change."[21]

Despite hostile threats, beatings by police, and the bombing of his own house, King and his loyal followers kept to their nonviolent philosophy and moved their case forward. In 1967, King broadened his campaign to concentrate on poverty issues and he soon became an outspoken opponent of the Vietnam War. In 1968, he went to Memphis, Tennessee, to give support to a strike by black men who hauled garbage. On April 4 of that year, he was shot to death by Earl Ray, a white man with hatred in his heart for blacks.

Although the civil rights movement has not accomplished all King had hoped for, tremendous strides have been made. We can trace the origin of these marching feet for social justice back to 1955, in Montgomery, Alabama, when the black people of the city decided it was more honorable "to walk the streets in dignity than to ride the buses in humiliation."

Thought to Ponder

Martin Luther King Jr. saw it was the right time to assume leadership of the civil rights movement when fearless Rosa Parks refused to leave her seat on that Montgomery bus. What "new thing" (Isaiah 43:19) is God calling you to perceive and act upon in your world?

Prayer

God of the future, give me fresh eyes to see the "new thing" you are doing in my own locale. Grant me the confidence to trust that though the way may not seem clear at the moment to accomplish this "new thing," you have proven again and again that you "will make a way in the wilderness and rivers in the desert." Amen.

WALKING ALONG THE SHORE
AT LOW TIDE

Rachel Carson (1907-1964)

The arrogant have hidden a trap for me,
and with cords they have spread a net,
along the road they have set snares for me.

PSALM 140:5

Rachel Carson started walking regularly in the woods with her mother at the early age of one. Together they explored the springs, flowers, birds, and insects. One day, her walking in the woods would challenge powerful industrial companies and lead to the modern environmental movement.

Born May 27, 1907, in Springdale, Pennsylvania, near Pittsburgh, the youngest of three children, she grew up in a modest farmhouse along the Allegheny River. She attended the Pennsylvania College for Women (now Chatman College) in Pittsburgh. Later, she gained a scholarship to study zoology at Johns Hopkins University, where she received her M.A. in 1932.

During her college years, Carson would return in the summer to find solitude in the woods on her long hikes. Originally, she had been an English major, wanting to be a writer, but then she met Mary Scott Skinker who taught biology at the women's college. Carson was so impressed with Skinker that she switched her major and eventually went on to graduate school, concentrating in science rather than in English. Carson and Skinker developed a strong bond and continued their friendship through the years.

The summer before Carson began graduate studies at Johns Hopkins she and Skinker spent time at Woods Hole, Cape Cod, at the Marine Biology Laboratory. Biographer Linda Lear comments on the startling effect the sea had upon her: "Rachel and Mary especially liked to walk along the shore at low tide, looking in the tide pools, finding new organisms among the rocks or clinging to the seaweed. Mary remembers that these excursions with Rachel had a 'mystical quality' about them."[23]

[Rachel] Carson has been called the mother of the modern environmental movement.

"Women in History"
www.lkwdpl.org

After completing her M.A. at Johns Hopkins, Carson desired to pursue a Ph.D. but was unable due to the economic depression of the 1930s. She could not even find a challenging job. Finally, Elmer Higgins at the United States Bureau of Fisheries asked her to write a few radio scripts on marine life for a program called "Romance Under the Waters." She worked in this government agency for fifteen years.

In The Writing Life, contemporary naturalist Annie Dillard explains her preparation for writing while living on Cape Cod. Every morning she would go for a walk, climb a tall dune, walk home again, slam the door, and begin to write.

Later in life, she reflected upon the turn of events that brought her writing skills together with her passion for science by saying, "I had given up writing forever, I thought. It never occurred to me that I was merely getting something to write about."[23]

In 1946, Carson and her mother made their first visit to Maine. They stayed near Boothbay Harbor and subsequently bought a cottage not too far from Southport. The beauty of Maine's rock coast overwhelmed Rachel and she wrote eloquently about her time in this place of tranquility. In 1952, she won the prestigious National Book Award for *The Sea Around Us*. Some scientists were skeptical of her because she was a woman, and she only had a master of arts in her field, but she had supporters too. This book, and others she would write, became bestsellers.

Not feeling well for some time, Carson had a physical examination late in August of 1950 and she learned that she had breast cancer. She realized she might not live long and in one of her letters she quoted Thoreau, "If thou art a writer, write as if time were short, for it is indeed short, at the longest."[24]

Even though she had suffered with cancer, she took on the biggest challenge of her life in writing the exceedingly popular but controversial book, *Silent Spring*, in 1962. She had always loved birds and as she walked in the woods in recent years she heard less and less birdsong. She realized something was wrong. Although she was aware that she would encounter fierce opposition from the chemical industry and other people with vested interests, she proceeded with her research and had her book published. She claimed that the use of DDT spray did "irrevocable ecological damage." Her enemies attacked her viciously, bringing up the old arguments that she was not qualified as a scientist, no matter how good she might be as a writer. Nevertheless, her book came to the attention of President John F. Kennedy, who ordered the testing of the chemicals mentioned in her book. As a result, many Americans have become increasingly apprised of the need for constant care of the natural environment.

In March 1964, Rachel had surgery at the Cleveland Clinic for her advancing cancer. During the surgery she had what she called a "resurrection," or an "out of body" experience. She exclaimed afterward, "Don't ever be afraid to die. It's beautiful."[25] Rachel died at her home in Silver Spring, Maryland, on April 14, 1964.

Rachel Carson's extraordinary writing gifts and her love of science and the natural world combined to fight social injustice. In particular, she questioned those who favored financial profits at the expense of protecting the world's natural environment.

Thought to Ponder

Many nets and snares were set to trap Rachel Carson in her efforts to preserve the natural environment against the threat of pesticides and other harmful chemicals. Nonetheless, she endured all these attacks and future generations are indebted to her. Do you think churches should use their considerable properties to provide habitats for birds and wildlife, nature trails, and wildlife sanctuaries? Why or why not?

Prayer

Lord, grant me the courage of my convictions to go against the crowd if necessary. Help me to pray the Serenity Prayer with understanding: "Lord, grant me the serenity to accept the things I cannot change, the courage to change the things I can, and the wisdom to know the difference." Amen.

"Penitential Walk"
to Sacramento

Cesar Estrada Chavez (1927-1993)

*When the days drew near for him to be taken up,
he set his face to go to Jerusalem.*

LUKE 9:51

Cesar Chavez, born on a farm near Yuma, Arizona, was influenced by his mother at an early age in the direction of nonviolence and morality. His grandmother thoroughly grounded him in the beliefs and rituals of the Roman Catholic Church. In 1939, however, his tranquil existence came to an abrupt end when his father owed money he could not repay. All his family's properties were lost. The entire family was forced to become migrants, working their way through the fields on their way to California.

Chavez, who stood 5 6 tall, was very shy as a young person and had painful memories of those years as a migrant. He would never forget the cruel treatment by the bosses against the Mexican-American people whom the bosses despised yet used to do work others would not do. Chavez was determined that some day he would find a way to ensure that his people would not have to suffer the degradation his own family endured.

Even in the classroom, Cesar was put down because he was a migrant, and he was severely punished if he attempted to speak Spanish at any time. When he was seventeen years old he enlisted in the United States Navy and served in the South Pacific during World War II. In 1946, after serving for two years, he was discharged and returned to his family in Delano, California. He came back to the fields, but this time he became active in the National Farm Labor Union (NFLU). Cesar was convinced that he could find a way to help his family and all Mexican-American people saddled with second-class citizenship. In 1948, he married Helen Fabela. In a relatively short time, they had eight children. Father Donald McDonnell, a Roman Catholic priest in San Jose, focused his ministry on helping Mexican-American migrant workers. He became a prime influence in encouraging Chavez to become a union organizer. In

Notably when Rousseau did walk, he was forced to move on his heels because of corns.

Joseph A. Amato
On Foot

addition, the young family man read everything he could find related to his dream. Louis Fischer's *The Life of Gandhi* especially moved him and provided him with guidance in accomplishing his goal; namely the use of nonviolent methods in effecting social change.

In March 1966, Cesar Chavez gained national attention when he led a grape boycott to bring to light the injustices of the largest growers in Delano: the Schenley Corporation, the Di Giorgio Corporation, Sand W. Find Foods, and Tree Sweet. He decided to lead a march from Delano to Sacramento to gain the support of Governor Pat Brown.

Chavez had used marches before to symbolize his cause but this time the march had a definite sacrificial aspect to it. In his own words, "This was an excellent way of training ourselves to endure the long, long struggle. . . . This was penance, because there was an awful lot of suffering involved in this pilgrimage, a great deal of pain."[26]

The small Mexican-American social reformer transformed the march into a religious pilgrimage during the Lenten season, leading his people on foot a distance of 250 miles to reach their destination on Easter Day. As the group marched through the San Joaquin Valley, singing and bearing witness, they attracted hundreds of workers who joined their protest. Chavez's recent biographers, Richard Castillo and Richard Garcia, elucidate: "After the first couple of days his old shoes gave him blisters and one of his feet swelled considerably. Since he considered it a penitential walk, he refused to take medication to lessen the pain." When the pain became too intense, a nurse forced him to ride in a station wagon, but "the next day he rejoined the marchers."[27] Before the demonstration ended on the steps of the state capitol thousands of protesters had joined the pilgrimage. The people celebrated together when they learned that a contract had just been made between the companies and the workers.

In the course of time, Chavez would lead other boycotts, not just for grape workers but also for lettuce workers and others. Although once in a while some of the Mexican-American workers would resort to violence in making their demands, Chavez remained committed to nonviolence. His

unexpected death in April 1993 shocked his people. No less than thirty-five thousand people paraded behind his casket for three miles to attend the requiem mass. This was quite a tribute to a man who rose from humble beginnings to become a sacrificial leader for his people.

Thought to Ponder

Cesar Chavez, in his marches on behalf of farm workers, identified himself with Jesus' journey to Jerusalem and his passion and sacrificial death. What sacrifice is God calling you to make as you walk toward your own Jerusalem at this time?

Prayer

God of grace, you draw near to me in Jesus, your Son, my Savior. Grant that when the time comes I will be able to make the sacrificial journey toward my own Jerusalem with the same firmness and determination that Jesus had when he set his face toward the holy city. Amen.

Stations on the Road to Freedom

Dietrich Bonhoeffer (1906-1945)

If any want to become my followers,
let them deny themselves
and take up their cross and follow me.

Mark 8:34

Dietrich Bonhoeffer, Lutheran pastor and theologian, was a striking prophet for his own time and continues to be a prophet to succeeding generations. Bonhoeffer was born in Breslau, Germany, in 1906, but he grew up in Berlin where his father was a prominent physician who eventually became the first to occupy a chair of psychiatry in Germany. Dietrich had a twin sister named Sabine. They were very close to each other in their childhood.

In Eberhard Bethge's massive biography of Bonhoeffer, he begins with a brief portrait of his subject. Among other things, he describes Bonhoeffer's walking style in this manner: "His movements were short and brisk. He didn't like leisurely walks."[28] Even as a young person he seemed to know where he was going and he was determined to get there with dispatch. In his early years he found walking to be a stimulus that renewed him in body, mind, and spirit. He always looked forward to the family tours that took him into the Harz, the Thuringian forest in central Germany. In those spectacular surroundings, he and his brothers and sisters hiked together.

The music legacy of the Bonhoeffer family continued when Dietrich's sister, Christel, married Hans von Dohnanyi (who incidentally also was hanged by order of Hitler). Their son, Christoph, eventually became Director of the famed Cleveland Orchestra and served from 1984 to 2002.

Sandy Mitchell
Your Guide to
Cleveland, Ohio

Bonhoeffer had a strong athletic body; he also was interested in music. Many of his peers thought he would pursue a vocation in music, however, even as a young person he was fascinated by the study of theology and theology won out. He studied at Tübingen for a year, but then returned to Berlin where he completed his education. He received a doctorate at the early age of twenty-one for his dissertation on the Communion of the Saints.

Reinhold Seeberg guided Bonhoeffer in his dissertation, encouraging him with his rich knowledge of church history and his special interest in Martin Luther. Bonhoeffer copied down endless quotations from Luther that he used freely in his subsequent teaching and preaching.

After graduating, Bonhoeffer spent a year as a pastor in Barcelona, Spain, but then returned to Berlin where he was appointed to teach on the theological faculty. In 1930, he spent a year at Union Theological Seminary in New York City where he became friends with Reinhold Niebuhr. While in New York, he developed a keen appreciation for African American life in nearby Harlem; in particular he immensely enjoyed the spirituals he heard there.

Upon his return to Germany, Bonhoeffer continued to lecture until the fateful day in 1933 when he was censored for criticizing the Nazi government. He was compelled to leave his theological post. He went on to serve as a leader of an underground theological seminary at various places, finally settling in Finkenwalde. Bonhoeffer's popular book *Life Together* comes out of this period when he taught and lived in close contact with young seminarians with whom he shared periods of intentional silence, Bible meditation, and rigorous theological study. Among Bonhoeffer's other significant books were *The Cost of Discipleship* (1937) and *Letters and Papers from Prison,* published after his death.

Although he visited Union Theological Seminary in New York City again in 1939, he refused to stay when war broke out in Europe. He felt his place was to be with his own people. Joining the Confessing Church, a minority of Christians in Germany who resisted the increasingly brutal Nazi regime, he moved closer and closer to defiant action. In April 1943 he was arrested along with his brother-in-law, Hans von Dohnanyi, both charged with being implicated in a plot on Hitler's life. Bonhoeffer was moved from one prison to another, finally winding up in a military prison at Flossenburg.

His letters from prison express a yearning for the days when he walked with family and friends in a more innocent time. On May 5, 1943, Bonhoeffer wrote to his parents from his prison cell, explaining to them his current practice of walking: "We are up fourteen hours, and I spend three of them walking up and down the cell—several miles a day in addition to the half hour in the courtyard."[29] On June 24, 1943, he wrote his parents again, "Just recently I discovered a tomtit's nest in the courtyard with ten young. . . . There is also a small ant-hill, and some bees in the lime trees. These things add a good deal of enjoyment to my walks in the courtyard."[30] Although he did not

Courageous Anne Frank also met a similar fate as Bonhoeffer under the Nazi purge of all undesirables. The "Jordaan Walk" in Amsterdam helps the tourist re-live those days. Rick Steves explains: *"This walk takes you from Dam Square—the 'Times Square' of Amsterdam—to Anne Frank's House, and then deep into the characteristic Jordaan neighborhood."*

Rick Steves
Amsterdam, Bruges &
Brussels, 2007

usually complain, on July 27, 1943, Bonhoeffer did write to a friend, "It's nice to have half-hour's exercise every day, but it is not enough."[31]

On June 30, 1944, he penned a letter to a friend recalling memories of a better day: "I can well remember how I longed to get out of Italy in June 1923, and I only got my breath back again on a day's ramble in the Black Forest, when it was pouring cats and dogs."[32]

Of course, Bonhoeffer's most memorable walk was the last walk he took to the gallows. In Bonhoeffer's writings on death he frequently used the walking motif. For example, in his "Stations on the Road to Freedom," appended to the *Letters and Papers from Prison,* he cited the value of discipline, action, and suffering. He then concluded: "Death is the supreme festival on the road to freedom."[33] But, it was not so much what he wrote that assured his place in history. Significant as that was, it was what he did that will always be remembered. He faced his death with remarkable dignity and courage.

On Sunday, April 8, 1945, only a few days before the Allied forces liberated the Nazi concentration camps, Bonhoeffer had just finished a worship service when the door opened. Two civilians entered the room and simply said, "Prisoner Bonhoeffer, come with us." Everyone knew what those words meant. As he was leaving he spoke his last words to a fellow prisoner, the Englishman Payne Best, "This is the end, but for me it is the beginning of life."[34]

The next day Bonhoeffer was hanged. He was a true prophet who declared God's Word to his own generation in word and deed, and his extraordinary example of the cost of Christian discipleship is a living witness for the ages.

Thought to Ponder

Dietrich Bonhoeffer taught by his words and by his example the meaning of the cost of discipleship. What specifically does it mean to you to be Christ's disciple in the world today?

Prayer

Loving and gracious God, may the cross of Jesus be central in my spiritual journey. Thank you for the indescribable grace you have shown in Jesus' life, death, and resurrection. When the day comes for me to face death may I do it in such a way as to bring honor to my Savior's name. Amen.

EXTRAS

A Program for Physical and Mental Fitness

Compiled by Rick Hasler

Check with your doctor before you begin any exercise program.

There are a lot of practical reasons for walking. Many of them are listed below. For people of faith, underlying everything else is the Pauline injunction: "Do you not know that you are God's temple and that God's Spirit dwells in you?" (1 Corinthians 3:16).

WHY WALK?

Walking:

- improves efficiency of the heart and lungs.
- burns body fat.
- raises metabolism, thus increasing calorie-burning even at rest.
- helps control appetite.
- increases energy.
- helps relieve stress.
- retards aging.
- reduces levels of cholesterol in the blood.
- lowers high blood pressure.
- helps prevent and control Type 2 diabetes.
- reduces risk of some forms of cancer (colorectal, prostate, and breast).
- aids rehabilitation from heart attack and stroke.
- promotes intestinal regularity.
- helps promote more restful sleep.

If that's not enough, walking also:

- strengthens muscles of the legs, hips, and torso.
- strengthens bones.
- reduces stiffness in joints due to inactivity or arthritis.
- relieves most cases of chronic backache.
- improves flexibility.
- improves posture.
- promotes healthier skin due to increased circulation.
- improves mental alertness and memory.

- spurs intellectual creativity and problem solving.
- elevates mood.
- helps prevent and/or reduce depression.
- improves self-esteem.
- increases sexual vigor.
- helps control addictions to nicotine, alcohol, caffeine, and other drugs.

THE 10,000 STEP CHALLENGE

The goal of the 10,000 STEP CHALLENGE program is to increase your awareness of the amount of physical activity you get in a day and then to gradually increase your daily activity level for a healthier you. The program guides you through eight weeks of activity.

During the first week, you will establish your baseline number of steps—the average number of steps you take on any given day. During the second week and each following week until the end of the program, you will increase your steps by 20 percent based on your personal goals.

What follows will give you the tools and information you need to develop your own personal 10,000 STEP CHALLENGE program. Once you have the habit of increased activity, you will not want to go back to being sedentary and losing the health benefits you are gaining. Enjoy walking and enjoy your health.

WEEK 1

Establishing your baseline steps

Depending on your activity level, your average daily step count could be 2,500, 5,000, 10,000, or more. (How far is 10,000 steps? If you have a stride length of 2.5 feet, then a 5-mile walk takes about 10,000 steps.) If you don't already have a pedometer—a portable, electronic device that counts the number of steps a person takes—purchase or borrow one. (See "Using your pedometer," below.)

This is not a race or a competition

Remember, the goal of this program is to identify your present activity level and gradually increase your activity level for better health and well-being. It is an individualized program and will give you personal results and satisfaction. Therefore, it is best to put on your pedometer each morning, reset the steps to zero, and forget about it until you go to bed each night.

Each evening, record the number of steps you take:

Day 1: _____   Day 5: _____

Day 2: _____   Day 6: _____

Day 3: _____   Day 7: _____

Day 4: _____

Add daily steps to find your total steps for the week: _____

Divide total steps by 7 for your average daily steps: _____

WEEK 2

Set your goal for week 2

- Increase your steps by 20 percent for week 2.

- Calculate your average daily step goal for week 2 by multiplying your average daily steps for week 1 by 1.20 (120 percent).

Average daily step goal for week 2: _____ (Transfer this number to the chart below.)

WEEKLY GOALS

Calculate your step goal for each of the following weeks. To increase by 20 percent each week, multiply the previous week's goal by 1.20.

Week 2: _____   Week 6: _____

Week 3: _____   Week 7: _____

Week 4: _____   Week 8: _____

Week 5: _____

KEEP ON WALKING

Increasing your level of physical activity is the goal of this program. If you are a 3,000-step-a-day person and you increase your daily steps to 5,000 or 6,000, you have done a great service for yourself. Keeping the increase throughout the year is an excellent accomplishment. Changing the habits of a lifetime takes time. Take small steps when making life changes. Small steps that turn into habits can reap long-term rewards.

IDEAS FOR INCREASING YOUR STEPS

Increasing your daily steps does not necessarily require a major lifestyle change. Try a few of these changes to your routine and see how many steps you increase each week.

At work:

- take the stairs instead of the elevator.
- use a restroom on a different floor or walk around your work area on your way back from the restroom.
- take a walk around the building during your break.
- take a longer walk at lunchtime.
- get up and walk back and forth by your desk if you have been sitting for 30 minutes or more.
- hand-deliver messages or papers.
- form a walking club with coworkers.
- park farther away from your building.

At home:

- take a walk each morning and/or evening. (This is the best way to add daily steps.)
- form a walking club with neighbors.
- make extra trips up and down the stairs.
- walk to the TV to change channels.
- walk down the hall and back during commercial breaks. (If you have a 30-second commercial, you can log 70 steps. But, better yet, turn off the TV and take a brisk walk around your neighborhood.)

Out and about:

- walk the mall before you begin shopping.
- park your car farther away from the door than you normally would.
- take a weekly nature walk at a city, county, state, or national park.
- walk in to the restaurant—avoid the drive thru.

USING YOUR PEDOMETER

The instructions that came with your pedometer will guide you through turning on your pedometer, wearing your pedometer, adjusting the sensitivity, replacing the battery, and troubleshooting. Pull out the insulation tab to activate your pedometer.

Pedometer tips

The pedometer measures movement. You will notice that it can jump several steps when you are bending, twisting, and so forth. This is normal. The calculations of 10,000 steps a day takes into account the additional steps from random movement. Your step calculations are based on your average for the week. Your individual stride, movement, or number of steps for any given distance will be different from any other individual. Use your pedometer reading as an average indicator of your daily movement. Though you can help motivate each other, everyone has different strides and movements so you can't really compare steps.

Don't forget to check your sensitivity setting

Make sure your pedometer is accurately recording your steps. Based on how you walk, you may need to adjust your pedometer's sensitivity. You can adjust the sensitivity of your pedometer +/-5 percent. Reset the pedometer to 0, then walk 100 steps on a level surface at an even pace. If the pedometer reads 105 or more, adjust the pedometer sensitivity button toward the negative indicator. If the pedometer reads 95 steps or fewer, adjust the pedometer sensitivity button toward the positive indicator.

Wearing your pedometer

Make sure your pedometer is securely fastened to your clothing. If not, you will have to replace a lost pedometer. Place the pedometer at waist level in a direct line with your knee. Make sure the pedometer is horizontal to the ground and the case is closed. If the pedometer is open or sitting at an angle it will not record steps accurately. Put the pedometer in place on your belt or waistband prior to pressing the reset button when you begin each morning. (If you wear a belt, place the pedometer on your belt as opposed to your waistband. Pedometers placed between your belt and waistband may not record accurately.) Record your steps in your workbook each evening before you go to bed. Reset your pedometer each morning.

Have fun!

There are always surprises around the bend.

A Spiritual Fitness Program from Linus Mundy's "A Guided Prayer-Walk"

from
The Complete Guide to Prayer-Walking, 151-155.
Used by permission of Linus Mundy

I have no doubt that you'll soon be looking for a T-shirt or sweatshirt that says, "I'd rather be prayer-walking," or one with a drawing of a pedometer showing 999,999 mile and the caption "and still prayer-walking." You will find your own right way to the enjoyment and rewards of walking meditation.

And yet I am often asked for more specific suggestions for a prayer-walking "style" or "system." So I think if this book is truly to be considered a "complete" guide to prayer-walking, it should offer . . . a "guided prayer-walk."

As we've said, walking is one of those exercises readily self-tailored for the individual. As human beings, we long for ritual, and as individual human beings, personal rituals are very important to each of us. Just consider the unique, "special" way you brush your teeth, butter your bread, prepare your morning coffee or juice or newspaper. But what may work for you may not work for me. Just the way my wife's "style" of reading the paper—very thoroughly and religiously—doesn't work for me (and my "style" of getting the kids to bed very unthoroughly and too unreligiously doesn't work for her!) we pray-ers and walk-ers want and need to have our own idiosyncrasies, our own rituals.

In this section of the book, however, I offer encouragement and specific help for those who want it: a sample or guided prayer-walk you might wish to adapt for yourself. Right away, however, I want to repeat: there is no "perfect" way to prayer-walk unless it's perfect for you and in your heart you feel it's "good enough" for God.

A STROLL WITH YOUR SOUL:
A GUIDED PRAYER-WALK

Step 1: Look up

A prayerful walk begins solemnly. Remembering that my journey is a spiritual journey demands that I look up and get connected with God on High. No, not a God so far away as to be unreachable, but on a lofty, exalted plane: within my consciousness and yet "beyond the within." As I prepare to take the first step I begin with a short prayer:

> *Guide my feet, O God. Direct me along your path. Teach me to walk more by faith, and less by sight. May my walk be to walk toward you, but even more importantly, a walk with you. Amen.*

Step 2: Look down

While I know that faith can move mountains, I also know that I need to be well-grounded here in the world I lie in. And so I pray:

> *Lord, let me realize that while I know I need to "look up," I also need to "look down" here on earth, lest I stumble and fall. There can be no serious commitment, no real relationship with this magnificent planet, until I abide with it a while and call it home. I remain a stranger passing through, until I decide for myself not just to pass through but to dig down and dig in. Amen.*

Step 3: Look back

Every journey toward something is a journey away from something else. We all carry a lot of baggage with us. (And some of it is good baggage, let us not forget!) As I walk ahead and meditate, I also look back, notice the footprints I've left behind, back where I've been, and remember, in prayer:

> *O God, keep me mindful of yesterday, but don't let me live there only. "Today has enough cares of its own," as Jesus taught. Help me to remember the times I thought I was all alone and suddenly found you there alongside me. Help me too, to know that whatever it is back there behind me on the trail—even if it's "gaining on me"—we can handle it together if it should catch up with us. Amen.*

Step 4: Look around

Here I am, at last, to the "main course" of the spiritual banquet. I am on holy ground now. (I was before, as well, but now I notice it!) And so I look around at all your gifts and life's possibilities; I look to the roads I've not yet taken, to the roads less traveled, to the hard roads that lead to change and challenge and you, and I pray:

> *What have I been waiting for? I know very well mystic Julian's prayer, "and all will be well, and all will be well, and all will be very, very well," but now I want to pray, "and all IS well and all IS well and all is very, very well." What makes it so? The company I keep and the Company I keep. Walk with me Lord, all the way home. Amen.*

Step 5: Look ahead

The perfect path, the perfect prayer-walk, takes us back to the beginning. And it leaves us refreshed. As I approached the end of today's trail I pray that God will take me deeper and deeper into the spiritual realm. I pray with Thomas Merton's *Thoughts in Solitude:*

> *My Lord God, I have no idea where I am going. I do not see the road ahead of me. . . . Nor do I really know myself, and the fact that I think I am following your will does not mean that I am actually doing so. But I believe that the desire to please you does in fact please you. And I hope I have that desire in all that I am doing. I hope I will never do anything apart from that desire. And I know that if I do this you will lead me by the right road though I may know nothing about it. Therefore will I trust you always though I may seem to be lost and in the shadow of death. I will not fear, for you are ever with me, and you will never leave me to face my perils alone. Amen.*

SIDEBAR SOURCES

PHYSICIANS AND NATURALISTS

Carl Jung
Laurens van der Post, *Jung & the Story of Our Time* (New York: Pantheon, 1975), 81.
Robert Strauss, *Adventure Trekking: A Handbook for Independent Travelers* (Seattle: Mountaineers, 1996), 217.

David Livingstone
Gary D. Yanker, *The Complete Book of Exercise Walking* (Chicago: Contemporary, 1983), 171.
Wendell Berry, "An Entrance to the Woods," *Recollected Essays, 1965-1980* (San Francisco: North Point, 1981), 241.

George Sheehan
Yanker, *The Complete Book of Exercise Walking*, ix.
Casey Meyers, *Walking: A Complete Guide to the Complete Exercise* (New York: Random House, 1992), 63.

Elisabeth Kübler Ross
Fergus Fleming, *Killing Dragons: The Conquest of the Alps* (New York: Grove, 2000), v.
Philip Ferranti, Cecilia Levya, with Joie Godkin, *Hiking: The Ultimate Natural Prescription for Health and Wellness* (Dubuque: Kendall/Hunt, 1997), 158.

Henry David Thoreau
Leo Damrosch, *Jean-Jacques Rousseau: Restless Genius* (Boston: Houghton Mifflin, 2005), 97.
Joseph A. Amato, *On Foot: A History of Walking* (New York: New York University Press, 2004), 6.

John Muir
Edwin Way Teale, ed., *The Wilderness World of John Muir* (Boston: Houghton Mifflin, 1954), xi.
Eugene Peterson, foreword to *Church: Why Bother? My Personal Pilgrimage* by Philip Yancey (Grand Rapids: Zondervan, 1998), 7.

Francis of Assisi
Rebecca Barnes-Davies and Jenny Holmes, "Living Lightly on God's Creation," *Presbyterians Today* 97, no. 4 (May 2007), 17.
Mark Bricklin, ed. *Prevention's Practical Encyclopedia of Walking for Health* (Emmaus: Rodale, 1992), 41.

Dag Hammarskjöld
Colin Fletcher and Chip Rawlins, *The Complete Walker IV* (New York: Knopf, 2002), 767.
Ferranti, *Hiking*, 30.

John James Audubon
Tom P. Hafer, *Faith & Fitness: Diet and Exercise for a Better World* (Minneapolis: Augsburg Books, 2007), 115-116.
Amato, *On Foot*, 134.

Roger Tory Peterson
Hafer, *Faith & Fitness*, 117.
Arthur Paul Boers, *The Rhythm of God's Grace: Uncovering Morning and Evening Hours of Prayer* (Brewster: Paraclete, 2003), 29-30.

POETS AND NOVELISTS

Johann Wolfgang Goethe
"Excursion to Weimar," www.middlebury.educ/academics/sa/germany/student_life/mainz/weimar.htm.
Sara Covin Juengst, *The Road Home: Images for the Spiritual Journey* (Louisville: Westminster John Knox, 2002), 44.

William Wordsworth, Dorothy Wordsworth

Leonard Sweet, *The Jesus Prescription for a Healthy Life* (Nashville: Abingdon, 196), 75.

Madeline L'Engle, *Walking on Water: Reflections on Faith & Art* (Wheaton: Harold Shaw, 1980), 196.

Wallace Stevens

Meyers, *A Complete Guide to the Complete Exercise*, 6.

Sam Keen, *Hymns to an Unknown God: Awakening the Spirit in Everyday Life* (New York: Bantam, 1994), 149.

Robert Frost

Phil Cousineau, *The Art of Pilgrimage: The Seeker's Guide to Making Travel Sacred* (Berkeley: Conari, 1998), 156.

Damrosch. *Jean-Jacques Rousseau*, 381.

Emily Brontë

"Health Hero: Majora Carter," *Prevention* 59, no. 6 (June 2007), 63.

Roland Bainton, *Here I Stand: A Life of Martin Luther* (New York: Mentor, 1955), 231.

Charles Dickens

Paul Simon, *Fifty-Two Simple Ways to Make a Difference* (Minneapolis: Augsburg Books, 2004), 80.

John Man, *Walk! It Could Change Your Life: A Handbook* (New York and London: Paddington, 1979), 16.

Jorge Luis Borges

"Attractions in Palermo, Buenos Aires, Argentina," www.enjoy-argentina.org/baires-what-to-visit-palermo-neighbourhood-attraction.php.

Charles M. Schulz, *Around the World in 45 Years* (Kansas City: Andrews and McMeel, 1994), 17.

James Michener

Rebecca Nelson and Marie J. MacNee, eds., *The Olympic Fact Book: A Spectator's Guide to the Summer Games* (Detroit: Visible Ink, 1996), 630.

Nelson and MacNee, *The Olympic Fact Book,* 584.

Robert Louis Stevenson

Arthur Paul Boers, book review of *A Spiritual Guide: Meditations for the Outdoors* by Bernard Brady and Mark Neuzil, *The Christian Century*, Jan. 10, 2006, 47.

Keen, *Hymns to an Unknown God*, 268.

Louis L'Amour

Juengst. *The Road Home*, 19.

Martin Marty, *Pilgrims in Their Own Land: 500 Years of Religion in America* (Boston: Little, Brown and Company, 1984), 430.

POLITICIANS & TEACHERS

Abraham Lincoln

Sweet, *The Jesus Prescription for a Healthy Life,* 74.

Man, *Walk!,* 213.

Theodore Roosevelt

Mort Malkin, *Walking—The Pleasure Exercise* (Emmaus: Rodale, 1986), 141.

Harry S. Truman

Bricklin, *Prevention's Practical Encyclopedia of Walking for Health*, 202.

Malkin, *Walking*, 126.

Hilaire Belloc

Cousineau, *The Art of Pilgrimage,* xxiv.

Rick Steves and Gene Openshaw, *Rick Steves' Amsterdam, Bruges & Brussels, 2007* (Emeryville: Avalon Travel, 2007), 26.

Alfred Kazin
Kenneth Cooper, M.D., *The Aerobics Program for Total Well-Being* (New York: Bantam, 1982), 129.
Patsy Cline, "Blues for Peace," www.patsy.nu/main.html, April 30, 2007, 2.

Clare Boothe Luce
Man, *Walk!*, 216.
James Harpur, *Sacred Tracks: 2000 Years of Christian Pilgrimage* (Berkeley: University of California Press, 2002), 180.

Arnold J. Toynbee
Fletcher, *The Complete Walker IV*, v.
Fred Miller, "Fair Street Cemetery, Sept. 28, 2004," *The Chronicler*, Winter 2005 (New Philadelphia: Tuscarawas County Historical Society), 12.

Frank Laubach
Colin Fletcher, *The Complete Walker III* (New York: Knopf, 1984), 3.
Linus Mundy, *The Complete Guide to Prayer-Walking* (New York: Crossroad, 1996), 20.

C. S. Lewis
Dale Bruner, www.fpch.org/dalebruner.htm, April 18, 2007, 1.
Amato, *On Foot*, 67.

Brenda Ueland
Amato, *On Foot*, 274.
Yanker, *The Complete Book of Exercise Walking*, 179.

PILGRIMS AND SEEKERS

John Bunyan
Ferranti, *Hiking*, 178.
Ambrose Bierce, *The Devil's Dictionary* (Cleveland: World Publishing, 1911), 254.

John Chapman, "Johnny Appleseed"
Yanker, *The Complete Book of Exercise Walking*, 180.
Bricklin, *Prevention's Practical Encyclopedia of Walking for Health*, 55.

Russian Pilgrim
Harpur, *Sacred Tracks*, 21.
Harpur, *Sacred Tracks*, 88.

Søren Kierkegaard
Joakim Garff, *Søren Kierkegaard: A Biography* (Princeton: Princeton University Press, 2000), 313.
Yanker, *The Complete Book of Exercise Walking*, 5.

Sadhu Sundar Singh
Robert Gilbert, Jeffrey Robinson, and Anne Wallace, *The Quotable Walker* (Halcottsville: Breakaway, 2000), 17.
John Woodbridge, *More Than Conquerors* (London: Moody, 1992), 151.

Thomas Merton
Henri Nouwen, *Walk with Jesus: Stations of the Cross* (Maryknoll: Orbis, 2004), 30.
Amato, *On Foot*, 56.

Mother Teresa
Mundy, *The Complete Guide to Prayer-Walking*, 163.
"Sister Nirmala," Missionaries of Charity, home.cncast.net/~motherteresasite/addresses.html, May 6, 2007, 2.

Toyohiko Kagawa
Strauss, *Adventure Trekking*, 194.
Fletcher, *The Complete Walker III*, 399.

Dorothy Day
Ira Rifkin, ed., *Spiritual Innovators: Seventy-Five Extraordinary People Who Changed the World in the Past Century* (Woodstock: SkylightPaths, 2002), 172.
Eugene Peterson, *Working the Angles: The Shape of Pastoral Integrity* (Grand Rapids: Eerdmans, 1987), 81.

Brother Roger Schutz
Richard L. Morgan, *No Wrinkles on the Soul: A Book of Readings for Older People* (Nashville: Upper Room, 1990), 125.
Woodbridge, *More Than Conquerors*, 302.

PROPHETS & SOCIAL REFORMERS

William Booth
The Salvation Army Home Page, "National News–Virginia Tech," May 2007, www.salvationarmy.org/inq/www_sa.nsf, 1.
Jerry Ellis, *Walking the Trail: One Man's Journey Along the Cherokee Trail of Tears* (New York: Delacorte, 1991), 3-4.

Mohandas Gandhi
Bonnie Stein, "Welcome to Racewalking and Bonnie Stein's Racewalk Newsletter!" May 2007, www.mindspring.com/~ronstein/index.htm, 1.
Rifkin, *Spiritual Innovators*, 59.

Harriet Tubman
Ellis, *Walking the Trail*, 255.
Sweet, *The Jesus Prescription for a Healthy Life*, 79.

George Macaulay Trevelyan
Fletcher, *The Complete Walker III*, 43.
Mark Fenton and David Bassett Jr., *Pedometer Walking: Stepping Your Way to Health, Weight Loss, and Fitness* (Guilford: Lyons, 2006), 64.

Bob Marshall
Strauss, *Adventure Trekking*, 10-11.
"Bob Marshall Country," gorp.away.com/gorp/location/mt/wild_bob.htm, 3.

Peace Pilgrim
Fenton and Bassett, *Pedometer Walking*, 12.
Los Angeles Times, December 3, 1973.

Martin Luther King Jr.
Robert J. Morgan, *Then Sings My Soul: 150 of the World's Greatest Hymn Stories* (Nashville: Thomas Nelson, 2003), 289.
Stewart Burns, *To the Mountaintop: Martin Luther King Jr.'s Sacred Mission to Save America 1955-1968* (New York: Harper Collins, 2004), 280.

Rachel Carson
"Women in History—Rachel Carson," www.lkwdpl.org/wikohio/cars-rec.htm.
Annie Dillard, *The Writing Life* (New York: Harper & Row, 1989), 26.

Cesar Estrada Chavez
Amato, *On Foot*, 108.
Paul Elie, *The Life You Save May Be Your Own: An American Pilgrimage* (New York: Farrar, Straus and Giroux, 2003), 429.

Dietrich Bonhoeffer
Sandy Mitchell, "The Cleveland Orchestra," *Your Guide to Cleveland, Ohio*, cleveland.about.com/od/music/a/orchestra.htm.
Steves and Gene Openshaw, *Rick Steves' Amsterdam, Bruges & Brussels, 2007*, 95.

NOTES

INTRODUCTION

1. Source information for brief quotations in this introduction by individuals whose stories are told in this book is provided at the point in the story where the full quote is reproduced.

2. Gene D. Cohen, *The Creative Age: Awakening Human Potential in the Second Half of Life* (New York: Harper Collins, 2001), 24-25.

3. Michael F. Roizen and Mehmet C. Oz, *You: The Owner's Manual: An Insider's Guide to the Body That Will Make You Healthier And Younger* (New York: Harper Collins, 2005), 305.

4. Ardath Rodale, *Gift of the Spirit: True Stories to Renew the Soul* (New York: Daybreak) 1997), 49.

5. Lou Holtz, *A Teen's Game Plan for Life* (Notre Dame, Ind.: Sorin Books, 2002), 25.

6. Daniel Pink, *A Whole New Mind: Moving from the Informational Age to the Conceptual Age* (New York: Riverhead, 2005), 68-69.

PHYSICIANS AND NATURALISTS

1. C. G. Jung, *Memories, Dreams, and Reflections* (New York: Vintage, 1989), 78-79.

2. Deirdre Bair, *Jung, a Biography* (Boston: Little, Brown and Company, 2003), 32.

3. Tim Jeal, *Livingstone* (New York: G. P. Putnam's Sons, 1973), 9.

4. Oliver Ransford, *David Livingstone: The Dark Interior* (London: John Murray, 1978), 84.

5. George Sheehan, *Running & Being: The Total Experience* (New York: Simon and Schuster, 1978), 163.

6. George Sheehan, "Foreword," in Casey Meyer, *Walking: A Complete Guide to the Complete Exercise* (New York: Random House, 1992), xiii-xiv.

7. Casey Meyer, *Walking: A Complete Guide to the Complete Exercise* (New York: Random House, 1992), 158.

8. Ibid., 158.

9. George A. Sheehan, M.D., *Dr. Sheehan on Running* (New York: Bantam, 1978), 44.

10. Elisabeth Kübler Ross, *The Wheel of Life: A Memoir of Living and Dying* (New York: Scribners, 1997), 33-34.

11. Ibid., 153-54.

12. Henry David Thoreau, "Walking," *Essays English and American, the Harvard Classics,* ed. Charles W. Eliot (New York: P. F. Collier & Son, 1938), 399.

13. Ibid., 395.

14. Ibid., 397.

15. Ralph Waldo Emerson, "Thoreau," *Selected Writings of Ralph Waldo Emerson* (New York: New American Library, 1965), 417.

16. Ibid., 421.

17. John Muir, *The Wilderness World of John Muir with an Introduction and Interpretive Comments,* ed. Edwin Way Teale (Boston: Houghton Mifflin, 1954), 17.

18. Ibid., xii.

19. Ibid., 124-25.

20. Ibid., xv.

21. Ibid., 311.

22. Ibid.

23. Elizabeth Goudge, *My God and My All: The Life of St. Francis of Assisi* (New York: Coward-McCann, 1959), 39.

24. Donald Spoto, *Reluctant Saint: The Life of Francis of Assisi* (New York: Viking Compass, 2002), 215.

25. Sven Stolpe, *Dag Hammarskjöld: A Spiritual Portrait* (New York: Charles Scribner's Sons, 1966), 22.

26. Dag Hammarskjöld, *Markings,* trans. Leif Sjöberg and W. H. Auden (New York: Knopf, 1965), 7.

27. Ibid., 58.

28. Ibid., 118.

29. Ibid., 116.

30. Ibid., 124.

31. Ibid., 122.

32. Ibid., 206.

33. John James Audubon, *Audubon, By Himself, A Profile of John James Audubon, From Writings Selected, Arranged and Edited by Alice Ford* (Garden City, New York: The Natural History Press, 1969), 12.

34. Richard Rhodes, *John James Audubon: The Making of an American* (New York: Knopf, 2004), 41.

35. Ibid., 87.

36. John C. Devlin and Grace Naismith, *The World of Roger Tory Peterson: An Authorized Biography* (New York: New York Times Book Co., 1977), 65.

37. Ibid., 199-200.

38. Jean Craighead George, *The American Walk Book* (New York: E. P. Dutton, 1978), xiii.

POETS AND NOVELISTS

1. Henry Thomas and Dana Lee Thomas, "An Adventure toward the Light—The Philosophy of Goethe," *Living Adventures in Philosophy* (Garden City, New York: Doubleday, 1954), 202.

2. Ibid., 206.

3. Nicholas Boyle, *Goethe: The Poet and the Age, Volume II, Revolution and Renunciation, 1790-1803* (Oxford: Clarendon, 2000), 564.

4. Nicholas Boyle, *Goethe: The Poet and the Age, Volume I, The Poetry of Desire, 1749-1790* (Oxford: Clarendon, 1991), 127.

5. William Wordsworth, *The Prelude: The Four Texts* (1798, 1799, 1805, 1850), ed. Jonathan Wordsworth (Hammondsworth: Penguin, 1995), 322. (Quotation is from the 1805 version.)

6. Hunter Davies, *William Wordsworth: A Biography* (New York: Atheneum, 1980), 70.

7. Annie Dillard, *The Writing Life* (New York: Harper & Row, 1989), 33.

8. Wallace Stevens, "Of the Surface of Things," *Collected Poems* (New York: Vintage, 1982), 57.

9. Holly Stevens, ed., *The Letters of Wallace Stevens* (Berkeley: University of California Press, 1966), 709.

10. Ibid., 744.

11. Ibid., 564.

12. Jay Parini, *Robert Frost, A Life* (New York: Henry Holt and Company, 1991), 215.

13. Louis Untermeyer, ed., *The Road Not Taken: An Introduction to Robert Frost, A Selection of Robert Frost's Poems with a Biographical Preface and Running Commentary* (New York: Henry Holt and Company, 1951), 271.

14. Jean Gould, *Robert Frost: The Aim Was Song* (New York: Dodd, Mead & Company, 1964), 100.

15. Parini, *Robert Frost, A Life*, 154.

16. Muriel Spark & Derek Stanford, *Emily Brontë* (New York: Coward-McCann, 1966), 46.

17. Katherine Frank, *A Chainless Soul: A Life of Emily Brontë* (Boston: Houghton Mifflin, 1990), 185.

18. Ibid., 11.

19. Charles Dickens, *The Uncommercial Traveller and Reprinted Pieces, Etc.* (New York: Oxford University, 1958), 1.

20. Peter Ackroyd, *Dickens* (New York: HarperCollins, 1990), 292.

21. Ibid., 678-79.

22. Ibid., 362.

23. Ibid., 511.

24. Brian Murray, *Charles Dickens* (New York: Continuum, 1994), 62.

25. Edwin Williamson, *Borges* (New York: Viking, 2004), 142.

26. Ibid., 381.

27. Ibid., 449.

28. John P. Hayes, *James A. Michener* (Indianapolis: Bobbs-Merrill, 1984), 4.

29. James Michener, *The World Is My Home: A Memoir* (New York: Random House, 1992), 411.

30. Michener, *Sports in America* (Greenwich: Random House, 1976), 551.

31. Ibid.

32. Ibid., 552.

33. Robert Louis Stevenson, quoted in *The Complete Book of Exercise Walking* by Gary D. Yanker (Chicago: Contemporary, 1983), 2.

34. Sidney Colvin, ed., *The Letters of Robert Louis Stevenson, Vol. I, 1868-1880, Scotland-France-California* (New York: Charles Scribner's Sons, 1917), 41.

35. Ibid., 245.

36. Robert Louis Stevenson, "Walking Tours," *Joys of the Road: A Little Anthology in Praise of Walking*, Ralph Waldo Browne (Freeport: Books for Libraries, 1970), 43.

37. Ibid., 47.

38. Ibid.

39. Louis L'Amour, *Education of a Wandering Man* (New York: Bantam, 1989), 124.

40. Angelique L'Amour, compiler, *A Trail of Memories: The Quotations of Louis L'Amour* (New York: Bantam, 1988), 138.

41. Ibid., 3.

42. Ibid., 105.

43. Louis L'Amour, *Education of a Wandering Man*, 210.

POLITICIANS AND TEACHERS

1. Carl Sandburg, *Abraham Lincoln: The Prairie Years* (New York: Harcourt Brace & Company, 1926), 77.

2. Ibid., 256.

3. Philip B. Kunhart Jr., Philip B. Kunhart III, and Peter W. Kunhart, *Lincoln: An Illustrated Biography* (New York: Knopf, 1992), 321.

4. Carl Sandburg, *Abraham Lincoln: The War Years* (New York: Harcourt, Brace & Company, 1939), 177-179.

5. Edward Wagenknecht, *The Seven Worlds of Theodore Roosevelt* (New York: Longmans, Green & Co., 1958), 15.

6. Theodore Roosevelt, *An Autobiography* (New York: Macmillan, 1916), 28.

7. Wagenknecht, *The Seven Worlds of Theodore Roosevelt*, 15.

8. Ralph Keyes, *The Wit & Wisdom of Harry Truman: A Treasury of Quotations, Anecdotes and Observations* (New York: HarperCollins, 1995), 156-157.

9. Ibid., 36.

10. Hilaire Belloc, *The Path to Rome* (Chicago: Henry Regnery, 1954), 49.

11. Ibid., 233.

12. Ibid., 70-71.

13. A. W. Wilson, *Hilaire Belloc: A Biography* (New York: Atheneum, 1984), 104.

14. Alfred Kazin, *A Walker in the City* (New York: Harcourt, Brace and Company, 1951), 104.

15. Ibid., 23-24.

16. Ibid., 106.

17. Ibid., 165.

18. Ibid., 176.

19. Ibid., 104.

20. Sylvia Jakes Morris, *Rage for Fame: The Ascent of Clare Boothe Luce* (New York: Random House, 1997), 79-80.

21. Stephen Shadegg, *Clare Boothe Luce: A Biography* (New York: Simon and Schuster, 1970), 187-188.

22. William H. McNeill, *Arnold J. Toynbee: A Life* (New York: Oxford University Press, 1989), 36.

23. Arnold J. Toynbee, *Experiences* (New York: Oxford University Press, 1969), 18-19.

24. Ibid., 28.

25. Karen R. Norton, *Frank C. Laubach: One Burning Heart* (Syracuse: Laubach Literacy International, 1990),13.

26. Ibid., 32.

27. Frank C. Laubach, "Letters by a Modern Mystic," *Man of Prayer* (Syracuse: Laubach Literacy International, 1990), 30.

28. Ibid., 33.

29. Clyde S. Kilby, *Christian World of C. S. Lewis* (Grand Rapids: Eerdmans, 1964), 23-24.

30. W. H. Lewis, ed., *The Letters of C. S. Lewis* (New York: Harcourt, Brace and World, 1966), 27.

31. Walter Hooper, ed., *The Collected Letters of C. S. Lewis, Volume I, Family Letters 1905-1931* (San Francisco: HarperSanFrancisco, 2004), 692.

32. William Griffin, *Clives Staples Lewis: A Dramatic Life* (San Francisco: Harper & Row, 1986), 396.

33. C. S. Lewis, *Surprised by Joy: The Shape of My Early Life* (New York: Harcourt, Brace & Company, 1955), 229.

34. A. N. Wilson, *C. S. Lewis: A Biography* (New York: Norton, 1990), 127.

35. Brenda Ueland, *If You Want to Write: A Book about Art, Independence, and Spirit* (Saint Paul: Graywolf Press, 1987), xii.

36. Ibid., 42.

37. Ibid., 42-43.

38. Ibid., 45.

39. Brenda Ueland, *Me: A Memoir* (Duluth: Holy Cow, 1994), 350.

Pilgrims and Seekers

1. John Bunyan, *The Pilgrim's Progress* (Philadelphia: John C. Winston, 1933), 7.

2. Ibid., 38.

3. Robert C. Harris, *Johnny Appleseed Sourcebook* (Fort Wayne: Allen County Historical Society, 1945), 8.

4. Karen Clemens Warrick, *John Chapman: The Legendary Johnny Appleseed* (Berkeley Heights: Enslow, 2001), 80.

5. Robert Price, *Johnny Appleseed* (Bloomington: Indiana University Press, 1954), xii.

6. Anonymous, "The Way of a Pilgrim," in Bernhard Christensen's *The Inward Pilgrimage* (Minneapolis: Augsburg Publishing House, 1976), 113.

7. Ibid., 114.

8. Ibid.

9. Joakim Garff, *Søren Kierkegaard: A Biography* (Princeton: Princeton University Press, 2005), 313.

10. Ibid., 310.

11. Ibid., 309.

12. Ibid., 311.

13. A. J. Appasany, *Sundar Singh, A Biography* (London: Lutterworth, 1958), 21.

14. Ibid., 27.

15. Ibid., 70.

16. Janet Lynch-Watson, *The Saffron Robe: A Life of Sadhu Sundar Singh* (London: Hodder and Stoughton, 1975), 147

17. Thomas Merton, *The Road to Joy: Letters to New and Old Friends*, ed. Robert E. Daggy (New York: Farrar, Straus, Giroux, 1989), 43

18. Ibid., xiii-xiv.

19. Thomas Merton, *Thoughts in Solitude* (New York: Farrar, Straus, Giroux, 1983), 83.

20. José Luis Gonzalez-Balado and Janet N. Playfoot, eds., *My Life for the Poor: Mother Teresa of Calcutta* (San Francisco: Harper & Row, 1985), 101.

21. Ira Rifkin, ed., "Mother Teresa," in *Spiritual Innovators: Seventy-five Extraordinary People Who Changed the World in the Past Century* (Woodstock: Skylight Paths, 2002), 184.

22. Mother Teresa, *No Greater Love* (Navato: New World Library, 1989), 171.

23. Keith Beasely-Toliffe, ed., *Living Out Christ's Love: Selected Writings of Toyohiko Kagawa* (Nashville: Upper Room, 1988), 44.

24. William Axling, *Kagawa* (New York: Harper & Brothers, 1946), 156.

25. Ibid., 166.

26. Ibid., 170.

27. Paul Elie, *The Life You Save May Be Your Own: Flannery O'Connor, Thomas Merton, Dorothy Day, Walker Percy* (New York: Farrar, Straus and Giroux, 2003), 46.

28. Dorothy Day, *The Long Loneliness: The Autobiography of Dorothy Day* (Chicago: Thomas More, 1952), 160.

29. Elie, *The Life You Save May Be Your Own*, 67-71.

30. José Luis Gonzalez-Balado, *The Story of Taizé* (Collegeville: Liturgical, 1990), 14.

31. Roger Schutz, *The Rule of Taizé* (Saône-et-Loire, France: Communauté de Taizé, 1961), 74-75.

32. Gonzalez-Balado, *The Story of Taizé*, 18.

PROPHETS & SOCIAL REFORMERS

1. Richard Collier, *The General Next to God: The Story of William Booth and the Salvation Army* (New York: E. P. Dutton, 1965), 22.

2. Ibid., 26.

3. Yogesh Chadha, *Gandhi: A Life* (New York: John Wiley & Sons, 1997), 125-126.

4. Louis Fischer, *The Life of Mahatma Gandhi* (New York: Harper & Row, 1950), 267.

5. Ibid., 367.

6. Kate Clifford Larson, *Bound for the Promised Land* (New York: Ballantine, 2003), xiii.

7. Ibid., 82-83.

8. David Cannadine, *G. M. Trevelyan: A Life in History* (London: Norton, 1992), 147.

9. George Macaulay Trevelyan, "Walking," *The Gift of Walking*, ed. Edwin Valentine Mitchell, (New York: Loring & Mussey, 1934), 57.

10. Ibid., 77.

11. Ibid., 79.

12. Sherry Devlin, "Bob Marshall: His Vision and His Legacy," *Montana's Bob Marshall Country* (Helena: Montana Magazine, 985), 79.

13. Ibid., 179.

14. Ibid., 82.

15. Peace Pilgrim, *Peace Pilgrim: Her Life and Work in Her Own Words*, compiled by some of her friends (Santa Fe: Ocean Tree, 1982), xii-xiii.

16. Ibid., 22.

17. Ibid., 73.

18. Ibid., xiv.

19. Martin Luther King Jr., *Strength to Love* (New York: Harper & Row, 1963), 139.

20. Martin Luther King Jr., *A Testament of Hope: The Essential Writings of Martin Luther King Jr.*, ed. James Melvin Washington (San Francisco: Harper & Row, 1986), 59.

21. Ibid., 60.

22. Linda Lear, *Rachel Carson: Witness for Nature* (New York: Henry Holt, 1997), 61.

23. Ibid., 80.

24. Ibid., 185.

25. Ibid., 479.

26. Richard Griswold Del Castillo and Richard A. Garcia, *Cesar Chavez: A Triumph of Spirit* (Norman: University of Oklahoma Press, 1995), 51.

27. Ibid., 52.

28. Eberhard Bethge, *Dietrich Bonhoeffer: Man of Vision, Man of Courage* (New York: Harper & Row, 1970), xxiii.

29. Dietrich Bonhoeffer, *Letters and Papers from Prison* (London: SCM, 1953), 15.

30. Ibid., 21.

31. Ibid., 23.

32. Ibid., 114.

33. Ibid., 163.

34. John W. Doberstein, introduction to *Life Together* by Dietrich Bonhoeffer (New York: Harper & Brothers, 1954), 13.